# NEW RIVER GORGE
## NATIONAL PARK & PRESERVE
### Visitor's Guide

**AMANDA ASHLEY & ROBERT LEGG**

Wolverine

# NEW RIVER GORGE NATIONAL PARK & PRESERVE VISITOR'S GUIDE

Words: Amanda Ashley
Photos, unless credited otherwise: Robert Legg
Design: Wolverine Publishing, LLC, and McKenzie Long at Cardinal Innovative
Published and distributed by Wolverine Publishing, LLC.
© 2022 Wolverine Publishing, LLC.
All rights reserved. This book or any part thereof may not be reproduced in any form without written permission from the publisher.

**Cover photos:** Robert Legg

**International Standard Book Number:**
978-1-938393-43-3

Printed in Canada

## WARNING!

# HIKING, BIKING, AND RIVER RUNNING ARE DANGEROUS SPORTS THAT CAN RESULT IN DEATH, PARALYSIS, OR SERIOUS INJURY. OPERATING A MOTOR VEHICLE ON STEEP MOUNTAIN BACKROADS IS ALSO POTENTIALLY DANGEROUS. READ AND UNDERSTAND THIS WARNING BEFORE USING THIS BOOK.

This book is intended as a reference tool for visitors to the New River Gorge National Park and Preserve. Both on and off the roads, the terrain of the park can be or is extremely dangerous and requires a high degree of attention to negotiate safely. This book is not foolproof, nor is it intended as an instructional manual. Some of the information may be wrong. If you are unsure of your ability to handle any circumstances that may arise, employ the services of local instructors or guides before trusting this book.

The information in this book is unverified, and the authors and publisher cannot guarantee its accuracy. Roads and trails can wash out or be closed for other reasons. Travel on any stretch of road, trail, or river described in this book, regardless of its description, may cause death, paralysis, or injury.

Please take all precautions and use your own ability, evaluation, and judgment to assess the risks of your chosen activities rather than relying on the information in this book.

The authors and publisher make no representations or warranties, expressed or implied, of any kind regarding the contents of this book, and expressly disclaim any representation or warranty regarding the accuracy or reliability of information contained herein. There are no warranties of fitness for a particular purpose or that this book or the information in it are merchantable. **The user assumes all risk associated with the use of this book and with the activities it describes.**

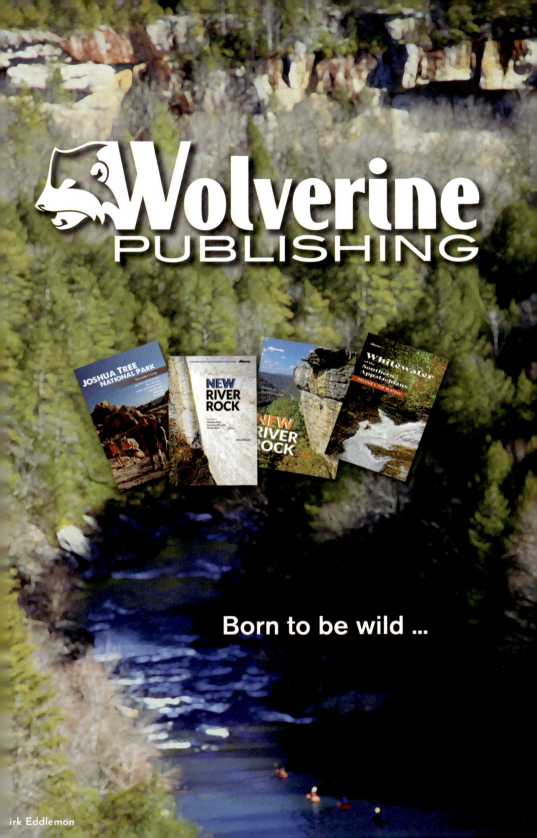

# Here We Go

**The New River Gorge is our hometown.** What makes it so special to us is not just its natural beauty, its recreational opportunities, or its small-town appeal. It's the people who live here, our neighbors and community. Throughout this book, we've highlighted a few of the remarkable locals — artists, entrepreneurs, athletes — who have built this vibrant community.

Our adventures at the New have been more than passing time and having fun. Done alone, or with family or friends, they're experiences and memories that have become the fabric of our lives. When we recommend a trail, a place to shop, or how to safely navigate cliff-top trails, it's because we've been there, done that, and half the time had some kind of epic doing it. When we recommend carrot cake from Cathedral Cafe it's not only because it is the most decadent, moist, flavorful carrot cake ever — it's also because it was our Mom's favorite and we'd do anything to share another slice of it with her. When we tell you how to drive on our country backroads, it's the way our Dad taught us how to drive here. (Lucky for you he won't be yelling at you if you take a turn too fast, or don't pull off the road for oncoming traffic.) Taking our kids to eat ice cream at Dairy Queen or the Stache in the summer, usually one of them crying, always melting ice cream everywhere, flies buzzing, maybe wasn't the funnest thing we ever did. But every time we pass that place we think of those sweet sticky little faces.

Our family has been here for generations, we know the kinds of memories you can make. Every time we pass a place we have a story that we share with our family and our friends, the kinds of stories that make you laugh and leave you feeling all warm and fuzzy. You know how it starts: "Remember that time …" We want you to be able to tell those stories of your own.

We hope our advice from experience makes your time at the New safer, less stressful, more enjoyable — but no less memorable.

*Welcome to The New. Do all the things, eat all the foods, have all the fun.*

— Amanda & Robert

**This book started out on Post-It notes**, a list of favorite experiences in the New. My brother, Robert, collaborated with me and started touring the park taking pictures. Within a few weeks we had a bloated mess of words and pictures. Connecting with Wolverine Publishing and Jeff Achey was a game changer. Jeff patiently got me organized as a writer, refined the concept and vision of the book, and together with Robert, and the Wolverine team of Jeff, Amber, Andy, and McKenzie, we created the book you now hold in your hands. We couldn't have done any of it without the tremendous support of our families and communities, and the knowledge and input from the folks who live in the towns around the New. So many people took time to talk through history, recreation, and every topic that is presented in the guide. Everyone I asked for assistance gave it. They shared their knowledge, their time, they answered the phone and returned the emails and we are so grateful for their contributions and support. Thank you to (in no particular order): Gene & Maura Kistler, Mike Williams, Bill & Ashley Chouinard, Mayor of Fayetteville Sharon Cruikshank, Kenny Parker, Jay Young, Karen Lane, Joy Marr, Holly Fussell, NRAC, Rico Thompson, Wendy Bayes, Melanie Seiler Holmes, Candace Evans, Bill & Sally Wells, Lewis Rhinehart, George Legg, Connie ONeal, Olivia Merritt, Alec Legg, Woodrow Ramsey, Amanda Mitchell, Bridget Stewart, Ed Wright, Tanner Robinson, Alex Wheeler, Kimberly Shingledecker, Erin Larsen, Adena Joy, Mike Masem, Sarah & Jeff Edwards, Elena Fauch Watson, Dave Bieri, Dave Sibray, Mel Lees, and Benjy Simpson.

This book is dedicated to those who wander and explore. The ones who drive the extra miles and walk the extra strides to see a new place, a new view, try a new flavor, or meet new people. The ones who hear the rustling of the leaves, the crashing of the water on the rocks, and the song of the birds. The ones who appreciate the beauty in the bend of the river, the slope of the gorge, and the changing colors of the sky. The ones who feel rejuvenated from walking on ancient trails, scaling cliffs, plunging through the whitewater, or simply sitting still in the depth of the gorge. The ones who find camaraderie in journeying with friends or much-needed solitude by solo travel. The ones who risk getting lost to find a new place, experience a special moment, and to make memories. **This book, reader, is dedicated to you.**

# Contents

## WELCOME  10

- THE NEW AT A GLANCE ................................................... 14
  - New River Facts............................................................ 15
  - Bridge Stats ................................................................. 16
- VISITING THE PARK ......................................................... 18
  - The New Is Located ..................................................... 18
  - Prime Times ................................................................. 19
  - Color by Rail ................................................................ 20
  - Seasonal Averages ....................................................... 22
- GATEWAYS TO THE PARK ................................................ 24
  - Canyon Rim .................................................................. 24
  - Thurmond Depot .......................................................... 26
  - Grandview .................................................................... 28
  - Sandstone .................................................................... 30

## REGION  32

- NATURAL HISTORY OF THE NEW RIVER GORGE ........... 34
  - Caution ........................................................................ 34
  - Geologic Highlights ..................................................... 35
  - Appalachian Riverside Flatrock Community ............. 36
  - Three Rivers Avian Center .......................................... 39
- REGIONAL HISTORY ........................................................ 40
  - Face in the Rock .......................................................... 41
  - Mary Draper Ingles ...................................................... 42
  - The African American Heritage Tour ......................... 44
  - Old Thurmond .............................................................. 46
  - The Battle of Blair Mountain ...................................... 49
  - Aerial Tour with Wild Blue .......................................... 50
- WELCOME TO THE 'VILLE ............................................... 54

## VISITING 56

- PLAYING IN THE PARK .................................................. 58
  - Spotty Service .................................................. 58
  - Pet Etiquette and Leash Laws ......................... 59
- SCENIC DRIVES ............................................................ 60
  - Adena's Advice ................................................. 62
  - NRG ATV ............................................................. 64
  - Country Roads .................................................. 67
  - Photography in the Park ............................... 69
- HIKING & BIKING ........................................................ 72
  - Going Further ................................................... 72
  - Beat the Heat .................................................... 73
  - Tough Footing .................................................. 74
  - Selfie Safety ....................................................... 76
  - Stay Found ......................................................... 79
- HUNTING & FISHING ................................................. 80
  - Survival & Bushcraft ....................................... 80
  - Leave No Trace ................................................. 81
- PADDLING & CLIMBING ............................................ 82
  - Whitewater ........................................................ 82
  - Water Levels ..................................................... 83
  - Rock n' Road ..................................................... 84
- ADVENTURES WITH KIDS ......................................... 85
  - Charlie Chipmunk ........................................... 87

## AMENITIES 90

- LODGING ...................................................................... 92
  - Cabin Fever ....................................................... 93
- STATE PARKS NEAR NRGNPP ................................ 94
- EATING .......................................................................... 96
  - Local Chef .......................................................... 96
  - Local Brews & Wines ...................................... 98
- GYMS, YOGA, & SPAS .............................................. 102
  - Energy Work .................................................... 102
  - Local Yogi ......................................................... 103
- SHOPPING, ART, & EVENTS ................................... 104
  - Mountain Momma ........................................ 104
  - Mountain Home Metalworks .................... 105
  - New and Scary ............................................... 107
  - Hank Williams' Last Stop ............................ 108
  - Mountain Sounds .......................................... 109

## RESOURCES 110

# WELCOME

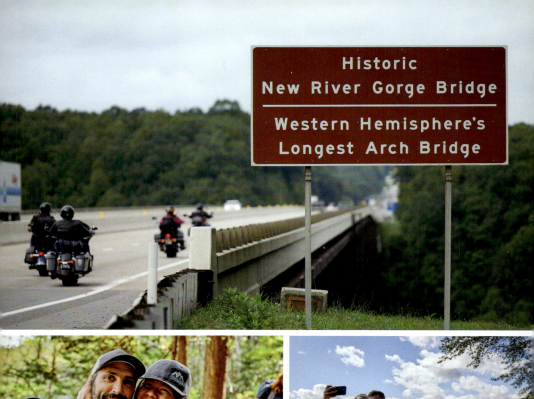

# THE NEW AT A GLANCE

**Originally designated as** a National River in 1978, as of 2022 the New River Gorge National Park and Preserve is America's newest national park, its 63rd. It is West Virginia's first national park. With this new recognition, the NRGPP (AKA "the New") is ready to prove what's already well known to many: West Virginia is definitely worth a trip!

Open 365 days a year, the NRGPP comprises the rims and canyons of 53 spectacular miles of the New River in southern West Virginia. It offers a unique variety of scenic and recreational opportunities, and is an epicenter of interesting regional and national history.

Unlike most national parks, there are no main touring roads through the park, and no entrance fee is charged. Instead, ordinary highways and backroads allow free and easy access, and the park proper is surrounded by small towns where visitors can stay, dine, and shop, while sight-seeing and enjoying the wide range of outdoor-recreation opportunities provided by the river, creeks, and forests. For history buffs, old coal-mining and railroad relics abound.

The park's features are quite spread out. The famous New River Gorge Bridge is the park's best answer to Yellowstone's Old Faithful or Yosemite's El Capitan, but most of the charm of the park lies in the nooks and crannies — a drive across the Fayette Station bridge down in the gorge, an unnamed waterfall in the woods near Fern Point, the not-for-everyone "stairmaster" trail down to the mining ruins at Kaymoor. Since there is no "main" entrance, having a basic understanding of the park's points of interest is essential for planning your visit. We have included several helpful maps in this book, and you can get the official park maps at the various visitor centers. For GPS navigators, note that the park has notoriously bad cell reception. Allow extra time for driving and exploring. Many of the backroads are definitely not suited for RV travel. No matter what vehicle you're in, use care on the narrow and winding roads.

The New has four visitor centers where you can get park information. From north to south, these are:

- **Canyon Rim** - Located near the north end of the Bridge
- **Thurmond Depot** - Down at river level, east of Oak Hill
- **Grandview** - An overlook area northeast of Beckley
- **Sandstone** - South end of the park, down on the river near I-64

## CULTURAL HISTORY

Though the New River Gorge region is a scenic wonder full of natural beauty, it is arguably even more interesting for its history. Native peoples were joined and largely displaced by waves of outsiders as early settlers, immigrants, and African Americans developed the area during the nation's westward expansion, bringing traditions, customs, food, music, and art from all parts of the world to create the distinct Appalachian culture found today.

The region's oldest archaeological sites date back 13,000 years to the Clovis civilization. There are 400 protected archaeological sites within the NRGNPP, with additional sites in the nearby Gauley River National Recreation Area and Bluestone National Scenic River. Especially notable sites exist at Mount Carbon and Glen Jean, both close to Canyon Rim. There is an excellent Native American exhibit

## New River Facts

- The New River originates near Boone, North Carolina, and flows through Virginia into West Virginia. When it joins the Gauley just upstream from the capital city of Charleston, both rivers lose their names and form the Kanawha, which eventually joins the Ohio River.
- The New is one of the very few rivers in the US that flows south to north, and is 320 miles long.
- The New's north-south orientation makes it a passageway for migrating animals and birds.
- Despite its name, the New is one of the oldest rivers in the world.
- The New (and the Gauley) features world-class whitewater paddling, and the cliffs of the gorge are almost as famous for their rock climbing.
- The New is the deepest and longest gorge in the Appalachian Mountains.
- The New is nestled within one the largest intact temperate forests on the planet, and is home to diverse populations of mammals, fish, birds, plants, and trees.

## Bridge Stats

Constructed of steel, the continuous-span, open-spandrel, arch truss bridge is the most iconic landmark of the Park. Carrying US 19 over the heart of the gorge, the bridge looms 876 feet above the New River, making it the third highest bridge in the country. Construction began in June of 1974 and was completed on October 22, 1977. Today, the structure remains the longest single-span steel arch bridge in the United States — its arch measures 1700 feet, while the overall length of the bridge is over 3000 feet. The bridge weighs in at 88 million pounds, which includes 21,000 tons of structural steel, 1700 tons of reinforcing steel, 6000 cubic yards of superstructure concrete and 17,000 cubic yards of substructure concrete.

at the Sandstone Visitor Center, where you can view artifacts and learn more about the ancient people who lived in the area. Remember that all artifacts and objects at the sites are protected. Leave them for others to discover and enjoy!

To explore the region's more recent history, you can visit abandoned coal works and railroad sites. Hinton's Railroad Days in October allows visitors to learn about the history of the railroad at the New, while the Nuttallburg Mine, down the secluded Keeney's Creek Road near Canyon Rim, allows visitors to glimpse the robust coal-mining industry of years gone by. Civil War buffs can explore the historic battle site at Carnifex Ferry State Park, overlooking the Gauley River just north of the park. Each year, the Appalachian String Band Music Festival, held at Camp Washington-Carver near Babcock State Park, celebrate the musical history of the area, featuring dulcimer, banjo, and fiddle.

## PLANTS AND ANIMALS

The NRGPP is home to over 1300 plant species, including over 50 rare ones. Many types of forests cover most of the landscape. The different elevations in the canyons, as well as the river bottoms and different sun exposures, give the park quite varied vegetation. As you explore, also keep your eyes out for wildlife. There are over 60 mammal species documented in the park, including endangered species such as river otter. The park is a popular birdwatching location, with bald eagles, great blue herons, peregrine falcons, and osprey frequently spotted. The 40+ reptilian denizens include several that might get your attention, including the usually docile but very camouflaged copperhead! In short, nature lovers will feel right at home at the New.

# VISITING THE PARK

**The New is easily accessible** by car, plane, or even train. Numerous cities fly to the small international airport in Charleston, the West Virginia state capital and an hour's drive from the New. The Beckley Regional Airport is less than 20 minutes from the Bridge and offers daily flights from Charlotte, NC, and Parkersburg, WV.

Trains departing from Indianapolis, Cincinnati, Washington DC, and Charlotte, NC, all make stops at the New, in Thurmond, Prince, and Hinton. Visitors who want to travel to the New by train will need to do some careful planning to get around once in the area.

Car rentals are available at the Yeager Airport in Charleston and in Beckley. While there is no public transportation system serving the NRGNPP area, Uber and Lyft are available, as well a local shuttle company, Hills to Hills Shuttle, offering airport transportation and scenic tours. Several major roadways bring you straight to the most iconic landmarks at the New. Interstates I-64, I-77, and I-79 make road trips fast and easy.

## The New Is Located

- **From the north**, 3 ½ hours from Pittsburgh on I-79 South, then US 19 (which takes you to Canyon Rim Visitor Center at the New River Gorge Bridge).
- **From the south**, 4 hours from Charlotte, NC, via I-77 North. From Atlanta, just over 7 hours via I-85 N and I-77 N. (These routes take you near Grandview.)
- **From the west**, 4 ½ hours from Cincinnati via KY-9 S and Louisville, KY, via I-64 E. (These routes take you past Charleston and onward to Beckley or Fayetteville.)
- **From the east**, it's just over 8 hours from New York and 5 hours from Washington DC, via I-81S and I-64 (which takes you first to the Sandstone Visitor Center).

### DRIVE TIMES TO THE NEW

|  |  |
|---|---|
| New York City | 9 hrs |
| Philadelphia | 7.5 hrs |
| Pittsburg | 3.5 hrs |
| Indianapolis | 6 hrs |
| Columbus | 4 hrs |
| Detroit | 7 hrs |
| Nashville | 7 hrs |
| Richmond | 4.5 hrs |
| Annapolis | 6 hrs |
| Greensboro, NC | 3.5 hrs |
| Knoxville | 4.5 hrs |
| Lexington | 4 hrs |
| Louisville | 5 hrs |
| Atlanta | 7.5 hrs |
| Columbia, SC | 5 hrs |

## WHEN TO VISIT

Whether you're looking for a summertime getaway or a winter escape, the New can fit the bill. It experiences all four seasons — wet springs, hot and humid summers, dry and crisp falls, and cold and snowy winters.

### Spring

**Flowers and Birds and the first events.** Each spring, the New region turns vibrant shades of green as the tree buds burst into leaves and blooming flowers color the landscape. The sun gets brighter, the days get longer, and temperatures begin to warm. Rain showers can be frequent, with layers of fog settling into the gorge, making for spectacular "mystic" views. The frequent rain often makes for exciting big-water rafting and paddling, even before the official high season begins on Memorial Day weekend. Spring also sees migrating birds fill the gorge, with over 100 species visiting the New as a crucial stopover. Look for colorful birds such as the scarlet tanager and blue-winged warblers. The annual New River Birding & Nature Festival, typically held the first week of May, offers a variety of daily birding tours — see birding-wv.com. The New River Gorge Festival, hosted by the ACE resort in mid May, features a weekend full of camping, outdoor fun, adventure films, live music, and more — see aceraft.com/event/new-river-gorge-fest. The trail running in the area is fun and challenging, and if running events are your thing, in late April you can test your speed and skill at the Babcock Gristmill Grinder, offering a half marathon and a 5K — see gristmillgrinder.com.

### Summer

**Whitewater, Hiking & Climbing, Music Festivals.** Summer in the New is the best time for getting on the trails, climbing, swimming, whitewater, and listening to live music in the mountains. The trails are typically dry, and hiking and biking conditions are comfortable. Summer rafting a great way to get cool while seeing the gorge from the bottom up. Early summer finds the rhododendron in full bloom, with pretty pink and white flowers all over the gorge — you can walk through the blooms in a "rhodo tunnel" on the Long Point Trail, emerging to great views of the Bridge and the gorge. For rock climbers, the many twists and turns

## Prime Times

**Anytime!** In summer, the park's most popular season, the New is one of the East's top spots for whitewater rafting. Hiking will be sweaty but pleasant, and a creek or river is seldom far away when you need to cool down. Winter often sees the gorge blanketed in snow, and is the perfect time to enjoy some quiet and beat the crowds. One of the best times to visit is when you can hike a rim trail or take a scenic drive to see the colorful fall foliage. The famed six-week "Gauley Season" draws whitewater enthusiast from all over the country. In mid October, BASE jumpers and spectators converge for Bridge Day, which brings hundreds to the park for one legal day of leaping off the Bridge — a spectacle worth seeing!

Jay Young

## Color by Rail

Not only can you get to the New by train, you can take a train ride through the Gorge. The Autumn Colors Express is a vintage passenger train offering roundtrips departing from Huntington, WV on select dates in October, offering the rail ride of a lifetime that combines spectacular scenery and railroad history. www.autumncolorexpresswv.com

in the river and the landscape make shade easy to find at cliffs like Junkyard and Butcher's Branch, or head over to the nearby cliffs at Summersville Lake where you can climb the rock, then turn around and dive directly into the lake! Summer is definitely "festival season," with the Waynestock Outdoor Adventure and Music Festival in Oak Hill, the Appalachian Festival Street Fair in Beckley, and the Mountain Music Festival at ACE.

### Fall

**Leaf Peeping and Bridge Day.** Fall in the New is spectacular as the leaves turn and the already magnificent views burst into full color. (Peak colors are usually around the second week of October.) Temperatures cool down and the humidity drops, making hiking, biking, and climbing even more fun. Rafting remains one of the top experiences; "Gauley Season" starts the first weekend after Labor Day and continues for six four-day weekends. The controlled release of water from Sum-

mersville Lake into the Gauley River creates dramatic flows and brings expert whitewater enthusiasts from around the world. Even if the Gauley's massive rapids aren't your thing, at the end of the day the excitement can be felt at the bars and restaurants throughout the area. Autumn excitement peaks on the third Saturday of October: Bridge Day. On this special day traffic is restricted on US 19, and the Bridge is open to pedestrians, vendors — and BASE jumpers. Hundreds of brave folks will huck themselves off the Bridge, then pop their parachutes, gliding expertly to a nice beach landing ... or sometimes to a big splash in the river! (Rescue boats await.) You can enjoy Bridge Day activities on the Bridge, on the water by rafting the New River, or hike out to watch the antics from Long Point. In between Gauley Season and Bridge Day there's the Oak Leaf Festival in Oak Hill, the last weekend of August and through Labor Day weekend, featuring parades, music, talent shows, cook-offs, plus the 38-years-running Country Roads Festival at Hawks Nest with bluegrass, country, and gospel music, food vendors, and apple-butter making. You can also stomp grapes at Daniel Vineyards in Crab Orchard and the Kirkwood Winery in Summersville.

## Winter

**Quiet time to get away and beat the crowds.** Winter is a quiet time to get away and beat the crowds. There's no better time to enjoy the stillness of nature than when it snows. Ice formations grace the cliffs in places, and winter is a great time to see the "bones" of the gorge. The absence of leaves opens up the views, allowing you to really experience the vastness of the terrain, and also reveals old mining artifacts hidden for most of the year.

The Bridge Walk, which is open year-round, is a great way to experience the winter views from the middle of the gorge. Hiking trails that are snow covered are great for snowshoeing or cross-country skiing. Trout are still active in the winter, and rabbit, grouse, duck and goose seasons extend into January and February, making fishing and hunting popular winter activities. Shopping at Tamarack is a great way to learn about West Virginia artists and craft, while touring the Beckley Exhibition Mine gets you out of the cold and riding through an old coal mine. In January Fayetteville hosts a Harry Potter-themed Wizard Weekend for wizards and muggles, complete with butter beer, quidditch, magical shops, and a scavenger hunt.

Bridge Day BASE jump. Jay Young

# Seasonal Averages

Summer months see average highs in the low 80s, with lows rarely dipping below the 60s during this time. Winter highs average around the 40-degree mark. The lowest temperatures typically hit around 19°F, which can feel even colder when wind chill and humidity factor in. Annual snowfall is around 48 inches for the area, so don't be surprised if you see some snowflakes during a winter vacation.

The park's nearest city, Beckley, receives an average of 40 inches of precipitation each year, with July being the wettest month, seeing over five inches of rain. Spring is also fairly wet, with May averaging nearly five inches of rain.

Knowing the forecast before you go can help you properly pack for your trip. Having some extra clothes and gear in your car that you don't use is better than being miserable and regretting the gear you left at home. Extra flashlights, sleeping bags, synthetic clothing layers, hats, socks, gloves, as well as emergency snacks, water, and beverages might save your trip.

### AVERAGE °F TEMPERATURES

| Month | High | Low |
|---|---|---|
| JAN | 36 | 23 |
| FEB | 41 | 26 |
| MAR | 50 | 34 |
| APR | 61 | 43 |
| MAY | 71 | 51 |
| JUN | 79 | 57 |
| JUL | 82 | 60 |
| AUG | 81 | 59 |
| SEP | 76 | 54 |
| OCT | 66 | 45 |
| NOV | 50 | 35 |
| DEC | 43 | 30 |

### AVERAGE DAYS WITH PRECIPITATION

| Month | Days |
|---|---|
| JAN | 13 |
| FEB | 14 |
| MAR | 18 |
| APR | 20 |
| MAY | 23 |
| JUN | 21 |
| JUL | 22 |
| AUG | 20 |
| SEP | 18 |
| OCT | 16 |
| NOV | 12 |
| DEC | 15 |

## WHERE TO STAY

Once again, unlike many national parks, the NRGNPP does not have the usual complement of official campgrounds and concession-run lodges within park boundaries. Instead, the surrounding communities supply most of the lodging options. Many hotel chains are represented in the larger towns such as Beckley and Oak Hill. Cozy cabin Airbnbs abound closer to the gorge. Developed campgrounds are found in the state parks and towns surrounding the park. If you are coming with a camper or RV, however, make sure you have a reservation, since RV camping is limited in the area. The Park does have a bit of free, first-come first-served primitive camping along the New River. Primitive camping areas have limited restrooms, no drinking water or hook-ups, and stays are limited to 14 days. Inquire locally for the best options.

Consider where you want to spend your time before you book your camp spot or lodging. Fayetteville is only five minutes from the Canyon Rim Visitor Center, for example, but 45 minutes from Sandstone.

For more lodging and camping details, see "Lodging" on page 92.

Here's to a New day!

## Food

Most people don't go to a national park for the food, but the unique interplay between the official park grounds and the surrounding communities make the NRGNPP a foodie's delight. The region's long history of tourism has led to much more diverse offerings than you might find in other parts of rural West Virginia, and the food scene here is ever evolving. One constant you will find in steady supply is that lovely hometown hospitality for which West Virginia is known.

When you come to the New, be sure to visit some of the old-style regional dining options found throughout the area. Enjoy a meal at Hawks Nest State Park's dining room with its fine river view. Dine at the historic Glen Ferris Inn next to Kanawha Falls, a spectacular site for fishing, SUPing, and kayaking. Up near the dam on Summersville Lake, stop in at Fat Eddie's for their charming Dairy Queen-esqe menu. Enjoy a fried green tomato sandwich at Tamarack, or a filet mignon at The Char, both in Beckley. Explore the regional variances in hot dogs while on a scenic drive along the West Virginia Hot Dog Trail, where you will learn what makes a WV hot dog truly unique. wvhotdogblog.blogspot.com/2021/07/the-wv-hot-dog-trail-new-river-gorge.html

For more cosmopolitan fare, the New has no lack of trendy eating establishments. You can find locally roasted coffees, decent bar food accompanied by great music, and diverse blends of casual to upscale settings serving highbrow creations of locally grown goods. From the iconic King Tut Drive-In, to Fujiyama Japanese Steak House, Cheddar's Scratch Kitchen, and the local favorite Dobra Zupas, Beckley can keep a foodie happy for a week. In Fayetteville you'll find delicious craft pizza at Pies and Pints, pancakes at Cathedral Cafe, breakfast burritos at Wood Iron, pub food and pool at Southside Tap House, sandwiches at Secret Sandwich, American cuisine at 304, and world cuisine at Wanderlust. For more food options, see "Eating" on page 96.

Visiting the Park 23

# GATEWAYS TO THE PARK

**The NRGPP has four visitor centers** that are key gateways to the New. Which one to visit depends on what you want to do. (If you stay for long, you'll likely visit all of them.) Here is a summary of what's going on at each.

## Canyon Rim

- Open year round
- Auto, RV, bus parking
- Cell signal, wifi, drinking water
- Wheelchair accessible, wheelchairs available, accessible restrooms, first aid
- Recycling and trash receptacles
- Picnic area, scenic overlook, trailhead, interpretive information, theater
- Maps, gifts, souvenirs, books
- NPS ranger or staff member present

The overlook at the Canyon Rim Visitor Center offers an exceptional view of the Gorge and its iconic bridge. You can also view films, museum exhibits, and find maps and books about the area. Located just north of Fayetteville, it is also the closest visitor center to some of the New's best hiking trails, including the 2.4 mile Endless Wall Trail off Lansing-Edmond Road, and Long Point and the Kaymoor trails off Gatewood Road.

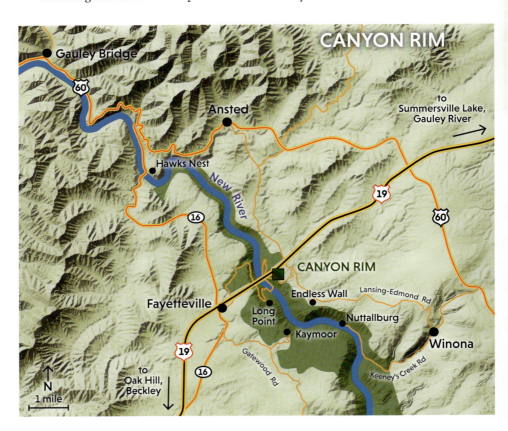

24  Gateways to the Park

   The town of Fayetteville is known for its cool vibe and small-town charm, and is packed with trendy shops, food trucks, great restaurants, two brew pubs, the Love Hope Arts gallery, whitewater rafting outfitters, as well as countless Airbnbs, cabins, small-chain hotels, and campgrounds. It's fair to say that it's the hub of recreation in the region. From the town park you can enjoy a paved walking trail and playground and access the town park trails, which connect to the Bridge Trail, the Fayetteville Trail, the Butcher's Branch rock-climbing area, the Long Point and Kaymoor trails, and the Arrowhead biking trails. These trails are also directly accessed from Gatewood Road, which continues to the Cunard River Access and the Cunard-Thurmond trail along the old railroad bed on the south bank of the New River.

Gateways to the Park   25

# Thurmond Depot

- Open from Memorial Day to Labor Day
- Auto parking — no RVs
- Cell signal, wifi, drinking water
- Wheelchair accessible, accessible restrooms, first aid
- Trash receptacles
- Picnic pavilion, playground, scenic view, trailhead
- Maps available

Located 9.5 miles from the town of Oak Hill, the Thurmond Visitor Center is located down by the New River in a restored railroad depot, featuring an information center and park store. Known for its river access, fishing, picnic area, birding, and riverside (first-come first-served) camping, Thurmond provides many opportunities for recreation and enjoying the natural beauty of the gorge. This is a must-stop for railroad and history buffs: the now quiet and preserved town of Thurmond was once one of the busiest railroad towns on the Chesapeake & Ohio Railway, and allows visitors to step back in time to when steel rails and coal were the region's driving force. Hikers can enjoy the Rend Trail, a 3.2-mile hiking route that takes you into the gorge through remnants of other old mining settlements.

Nearby Oak Hill is well known for its walkability, paved rail-trail, Main Street charm, and easy access to the park. It is home to Pin Heads Bowling Alley, the Fayette County Farmers Market, several whitewater outfitters, and the Summit Bechtel Reserve, home to the National Scout Jamboree and an adventure and scouting training center for the Boy Scouts of America.

26  Gateways to the Park

# Grandview

- Open from Memorial Day to Labor Day; grounds open year-round
- Auto, RV, bus parking
- Wheelchair accessible, accessible restrooms, first aid
- Recycling and trash receptacles
- Picnic pavilion, playground, overlooks, trailhead
- Maps, gifts, souvenirs, books
- NPS ranger or staff member present

About a 12-mile drive east of Beckley, the Grandview Visitor Center is open June through August, although the park grounds are open year-round. A popular destination for sightseeing, hiking, and a top picnic spot, Grandview has some of the most spectacular scenery in the park. Ranger-led talks and walks, playgrounds, and hiking trails are popular attractions. Located at the deepest part of the gorge, the main overlook is 1400 feet above the river; visitors can see seven miles of the New River, including the old

28   Gateways to the Park

mining townsite of Quinnimont, which in 1873 sent out the region's first shipment of coal. The North and Turkey Spur overlooks provide quite different views. With over six miles of hiking trails of various difficulty, there is a stroll here for everyone, and it's one of the most popular places to view the rhododendron bloom. Grandview also features Theater West Virginia, where you can enjoy outdoor plays throughout the summer.

As West Virginia's eighth largest city, nearby Beckley is known as an art and entertainment center. It is home to Tamarack, West Virginia's premier showcase of Appalachian arts and crafts, and the Beckley Exhibition Coal Mine. Much of Beckley's early history is rooted in mining, and it's often called the Smokeless Coal Capital.

Beckley has plenty of amenities to offer park visitors. In addition to the chain-hotels, you can find treehouse and cabin rentals. Alpine Ministries, located nine miles north of Beckley in Mount Hope, is a faith-based outfitter offering whitewater tours and adventure trips. In addition to the usual chain restaurants, there are plenty of dining options — Dobra Zupas is a local favorite, serving gourmet craft food and craft beer in a relaxed atmosphere. The Resort at Glade Springs features a golf course, spa, and many event venues in addition to fine and casual dining and lodging options. Winter-sports enthusiasts will also enjoy making turns at Winterplace Ski Resort, about 15 miles south down I-77.

# Sandstone

- Open spring, summer, fall, plus limited winter hours
- Auto, RV, bus parking, bike racks
- Cell signal, wifi, drinking water
- Wheelchair accessible, wheelchairs available, accessible restrooms, first aid
- Recycling and trash receptacles
- Picnic pavilion, trailhead, interpretive information, theater
- Maps, gifts, souvenirs, books
- NPS ranger or staff member present

Just north of I-64 (Exit 139), along Route 20, the Sandstone Visitor Center is the gateway to the park's only scenic riverside drive, which you will take if you want to visit the actual falls area (about a half-hour drive from the visitor center). Tucked in the southern corner of the park, farthest upstream, the Sandstone area features the remarkable Sandstone Falls, the first and largest of the falls and rapids on the New River, marking the transition of the river from a broad, gentle, flatlands waterway to a swift, rapids-filled beast in the precipitous New River Gorge proper. There are several short trails, boardwalks, and river-access points here. The falls themselves are impressive not for their height but for their breadth — they're 1500 feet wide, divided by a series of islands as the shallow river drops 25 feet. The water looks gentle but the current can be dangerously swift; the NPS recommends always wearing a life jacket when recreating near Sandstone Falls — for good reason! Other Sandstone features include a native-plant garden, bookstore,

30  Gateways to the Park

exhibits, and park films. Due to the milkweed in the native garden, Sandstone is registered as a monarch butterfly waystation, and visitors can observe the butterflies, caterpillars, and chrysalis' in the plants around the center.

Nearby Hinton is known for its historic district, quaint downtown full of shops and restaurants, and railroad museum. In Talcot, 11 miles from Hinton, is the John Henry Historical Park at the Great Bend Tunnel, honoring the legendary Black railroad steel driver and his feats of strength and determination. You can catch a movie in the Ritz Theater, built in 1929, before grabbing a bite to eat at the award-winning The Market at Courthouse Square, featuring all-day breakfast and sandwiches. You can camp or rent cabins in nearby Bluestone State Park, or enjoy the spa, lodge, and RV camping at Pipestem State Park. On the way between Hinton and Sandstone, don't miss the Sandstone Falls Overlook for a view of the falls from 600 feet above.

# REGION

# NATURAL HISTORY OF THE NEW RIVER GORGE

**The New River Gorge** may be a new national park, but its history is eons old. This much-loved feature of West Virginia's landscape is the result of millions of years of erosion by the waters of the river. Although some geologists disagree, it appears that the New may be one of the oldest rivers in the world. Remarkably, from its origins south and east of the park, the New River actually cuts westward right through the crest of the Appalachian Mountains — it's the only river to do so. Within the park, on the Appalachian Plateau, the gorge reaches 1000 feet deep. The age and depth of the gorge have made it an important migratory pathway for plants and animals, connecting coastal ecosystems with those of the Midwest and creating many microclimates that have allowed diverse species to evolve or survive.

## GEOLOGY

Despite its name, the New River is anything but. In fact, most geologists think it's more ancient than "old" rivers such as the Nile, the Rhine, and the Colorado. Some scientists estimate the New River at approximately 360 million years old, the present-day remnant of an extinct river known as the Teays, which was partially obliterated by glaciers during past ice ages. This means that the river originated during the Carboniferous Period, a time when coal was first beginning to form and the very first reptiles appeared on Earth.

### Caution

Visitors without technical rock-climbing experience should (carefully!) admire the cliffs from the overlooks and not attempt the very dangerous climbing-access routes! Never throw rocks, sticks, or any items from cliff tops — rock climbers are very likely active below!

Other scientists, notably the West Virginia Geological & Economic Survey team, suggest a younger river, from between just 3 to 320 million years, depending on the dating method used. Specifically, the WVG&ES proposes five different manners of calculating the river's age:

- The river cuts through rocks 320 million years old, which are the most recent found in the region. Thus, the river could only be 320 million years old at the most.
- If the river formed at the same time as the Appalachian Mountains, that would make it about 225 million years old.
- If the river formed during the most recent Appalachian Mountain shifting, the river's age would more likely be 65 million years.
- The current depth of the New's canyons divided by the universal average erosion rate would suggest an age of about 10 million years.
- Using the Grand Canyon's age as a reference, the extent of the New River's erosion in comparison implies that the New River is only about 3 million years old.

As with many topics in geology, the debate continues!

While the full length of the New River is 320 miles, only 66 miles pass through the park — from Hinton in the south to Hawks Nest Dam in the north. The southernmost portion of the park is upstream of the gorge proper, and here the river flows through a gentler landscape of hills and open valleys. At Sandstone Falls, the action picks up and the river drops an average of 11 feet per mile. On average, the New River flows at a speed between 3.5 mph and 7 mph, carrying about 9000 cubic feet of water per second (cfs), with occasional high-water episodes of over 200,000 cfs.

A widely discussed anomaly about the New River is that while most rivers in the U.S. run from north to south, the New runs south to

# Geologic Highlights

Mike Williams

While you're visiting the park, you can stop by certain landmarks to get a better view of the geologic past and present.

**View Gorgeous Sandstone Falls**
Not only is Sandstone Falls a beautiful place to view the rushing river, but it's also geologically interesting. Here, the main flow of the river abruptly drops 25 feet over a ledge of erosion-resistant Stony Gap Sandstone. At Sandstone Falls, visitors will notice that the New River begins to narrow (and thus, move faster) as it flows away from the gentle bottomlands and enters the mountains.

**Observe Climbers on the Endless Wall**
Nuttall Sandstone makes up the Endless Wall, named by rock climbers since, unlike most sheer cliffs, it runs unbroken by low-angle areas for almost three miles. The cliffs reach 150 feet tall in spots and are dead-vertical or even slightly overhanging. Visitors who enjoy rock climbing or watching climbers can visit Endless Wall to see the sandstone up close. To get to the rim, use either the Fern Creek Trailhead or the Nuttall Trailhead along the Lansing-Edmond Road. Caution: do not attempt to descend the climbing-access ladders if you are not a technical rock climber with the appropriate gear and experience!

**Experience the Power of the River**
Want to get a feel for the erosional power of the New River? Paddle its whitewater! Access the river near Cunard (for a six-mile trip) or Thurmond (for a 13-mile trip) and paddle your way to Fayette Station through the strong waters that have helped create the beautiful landscape we see today. Depending on the water level, this is a challenging to experts-only whitewater run, but the many local guide services will be happy to let novices experience the waves.

**Understand the Coal**
Visit the Beckley Exhibition Coal Mine, where you can tour an old mine. You'll also get the chance to see the coal camp which includes a restored church and school. For the more adventurous hiking trails, visit the gorge's mining sites. See page 72 for our recommended hikes.

## Appalachian Riverside Flatrock Community

The New River Gorge is home to a special type of ecosystem regional biologists call the Appalachian Riverside Flatrock Community. Here, a variety of plants grow that haven't been established elsewhere in the region. They are specifically adapted to the unique conditions of the river, which historically, has flooded repeatedly.

When the floods wash away the soil, most plants can't survive, and therefore, lichen takes over, which eventually helps create small amounts of soil. This soil creates conditions that smaller plants can grow and which ultimately are succeeded by larger ones with more complex root systems, such as red cedar and scrub pines.

To see an example of an Appalachian Riverside Flatrock Community, head over to the Camp Brookside Environmental Education Center on Mullens Road near Hinton. Sandstone Falls also accommodates several Appalachian Riverside Flatrock Communities.

north. While this isn't unheard of among rivers (and doesn't mean the water runs uphill, as it appears on a map!), it does make the New River that much more unusual and interesting — especially since it cuts through the East's main mountain chain to follow this course.

As with most landforms, the rocks of the New River Gorge are layered, with the oldest rocks at the bottom. While the deepest part of the canyon is 1600 feet, in some parts of the gorge the strata are so steeply tilted that the exposed rock layers are 4000 feet thick, a testament to the incredible amount of time that went into the region's geologic development, slowly compressing mud, silt, sand, and various kinds of organic material to form the layers of sandstones and shales — and coal — that exist today.

The exposed rocks in the park are almost exclusively of the Carboniferous Period, about 300 to 350 million years (MY) old. The oldest rocks are in the southern park (near Sandstone), including various formations of Mississippian age (360-325 MY old), mostly non-marine shale, but with some thin limestone beds as well as the Stony Gap Sandstone that forms Sandstone Falls. In the north (Canyon Rims) region, the exposed rocks are slightly younger, from the Pennsylvanian sub-period (325-300 MY old). These include all the coal-bearing rocks in the gorge, as well as the distinctive Nuttall Sandstone cliff band near the gorge rim that is so prominent from the Fayetteville-area overlooks. Composed of 98% quartz and very hard, Nuttall Sandstone is prized by rock climbers. For decades beginning in the 1870s, coal was heavily mined in the New River Gorge. The region's unusually pure coal was prized for its "smokeless," clean-burning properties (relatively speaking!). One good place to view the Sewell coal seam is Nuttallburg, a ghost town down the Keeney's Creek Road.

## FLORA

The flora of the New River Gorge is the most varied and diverse of any river gorge in the central or southern Appalachians. From grassy bottomlands to high mountaintops, each location of the New River Gorge has something special to offer.

Five out of the six southeastern forest communities can be found here, meaning the park is basically a one-stop shop for all your tree needs. Since each tree species thrives in different conditions, it's helpful to know a bit about each. Areas that see frequent flooding, like riverbanks, are often home to sycamores and river birch. Oaks and hickories, on the other hand, typically prefer drier and sunnier habitats. Scrub pines favor dry places that have been the site of wildfires. The visitor center can offer more detailed guides to the park's flora — over 1300 species occur here! — but here are a few highlights.

## Rhododendron

Spring and early summer in the New River Gorge is a lovely time for many reasons, including the blooming of two species of brightly colored rhododendrons. These shrubs favor shaded areas, so look for them growing under tall trees or in ravines near the river. The great rhododendron, deemed West Virginia's state flower in the early 1900s, exhibits clusters of white flowers and has long leaves that are slightly pointed at the ends. Some locals call this plant "great laurel." The Catawba rhododendron, in contrast, exhibits clusters of pink or purple flowers. Some people refer to it as rosebay or purple laurel. To see rhododendrons blooming, you'll need to visit in June or July.

## Mountain Laurel

This plant looks like a smaller version of rhododendron, with smaller, pointier leaves. Visit in May, June, or July for your best chances of seeing it in bloom. Mountain laurel grows best at higher altitudes, so try scanning the higher slopes or stopping at an overlook like Grandview.

## Oak

Known for their acorns and lobed leaves, the sturdy oaks are one of the most common tree groups in the NRGNPP, so you'll likely find yourself surrounded by them no matter where you are. The red oak is distinctive for its bright red leaves during autumn. Chinquapin oaks are also prevalent in some parts of the park, including the end of the Stone Cliff Trail. These oaks are noteworthy for their sweet-tasting acorns which are consumed by not just squirrels and birds but humans as well.

## Mushrooms

The New River Gorge is home to many varieties of mushrooms. Keep in mind that some mushrooms are extremely toxic, so don't attempt to touch any of them. Some frequently sighted mushrooms in the area include morels, a variety that is covered in thin ridges, and wood ear, which ... resembles an ear. Take a look around Fern Creek on the Endless Wall hiking trail. The moist ground conditions from the creek in fall and spring give rise to several types of mushrooms that make for beautiful photographs.

# FAUNA

One of the best parts of visiting any national park is getting the chance to see wildlife in its natural habitat. Keep in mind that it is in both the animals' best interest and yours to maintain a safe distance. Never feed wildlife — rather than benefitting them, human food disrupts the animal's natural behavior and makes them less effective at finding their own food.

## Black bear

A black bear sighting in the wild is likely at the New! Male bears in the area usually weigh around 250 pounds, while females are smaller, at around 100 pounds. Black bears eat mostly plants (including having a soft spot for berries), but will eat carrion and of course honey. Black bears are generally less aggressive than the grizzlies found in some parks out West, but they are potentially dangerous and it's important to keep your distance. Mother bears with young cubs are extremely protective and should be treated with extra caution.

## Bobcat

You're around the campfire after dark and see a pair of yellow eyes staring back at you — there's a chance those eyes belong to the famed bobcat, a feline with a very short ("bobbed") tail. Around two feet tall and up to four feet long, the bobcat feeds mostly on eastern cottontails, rodents, and birds. Bobcats normally aren't aggressive toward humans. It's not common to see them since they are nocturnal and tend to avoid human contact. You are more likely to see their tracks along hiking trails, perhaps in the mud near the river around Thurmond.

## White-Tailed Deer

This is one of the most common animals to spot in the park. The white patch beneath its tail might catch your eye, while the rest of the body is reddish-brown in spring and summer, turning a darker grayish brown during the cooler months. Your best chances for spotting white-tailed deer are during dusk and dawn when they are foraging on trees and shrubs. Midday the deer typically sleep, making them difficult to spot. You may find antlers shed on the forest ground during the early months of the year (January through March), but remember that park regulations prohibit the removal of any natural objects to preserve the entirety of the ecosystem.

## Red fox

These attractive canines are identifiable by their brightly colored coats. Red foxes enjoy a mixed diet of berries, rodents, squirrels, and reptiles. These creatures can often be sighted roaming in open fields. Like most of the park's animals, foxes are most often sighted just before sunrise or in the late evening.

## Black rat snake

When you're walking along a trail and hear a rustling in the leaves or grass, you might be in the presence of a black rat snake. But don't worry — this species of snake isn't poisonous. Regularly seen along the hiking trails, this mostly black snake has a white chin and underbelly. The snake's size may startle you — they're often up to six feet long! If you're hoping to spot one of these lovely reptiles, don't forget to look up. Their climbing ability is their main claim to fame, and you just might see one hanging out in a tree limb.

## Bats

Thanks to its abundant abandoned mines, the New River Gorge is a virtual bat haven. Two species of the 10 types of bats that have been observed here are endangered, including the Virginia big-eared bat, characterized by its inch-long ears. These bats often hibernate in limestone caves, and if disturbed during this period may abandon their offspring. The park's other endangered bat species is the Indiana bat, which typically grows to just an inch or two long. Check out the "bat condo" (created by the NPS) in Grandview for a chance to see the more common brown bat on summer evenings — up to 10,000 bats may be in residence!

## Bald Eagles

Everyone can identify these iconic birds with their white heads and tails contrasting starkly with their dark brown bodies. Formerly endangered, these birds have increased in number thanks to major conservation efforts over the decades. At the park, visitors may catch an occasional sighting of this beloved bird, which is an expert fisher. Bald eagles choose especially tall trees to construct their nests, safely away from predators. The park's best-known nest site is at Brooks Island, near Sandstone Falls.

Eastern bluebird. 📷 Louise McLaughlin

## Red-Tail Hawks

If you love watching birds of prey soar through the skies, keep an eye out for the beautiful red-tail hawk, readily recognized by the reddish hue of the top of its tail feathers visible as the hawk circles. Red-tail hawks prey primarily on small rodents, although it's not unusual for them to eat lizards, other birds, grasshoppers, and even fish. To spot a red-tail, scan the trees and other high locations. These birds are known for perching for hours to wait for a field mouse to make a wrong move.

## Peregrine Falcons

Peregrine falcon populations declined sharply due to DDT pesticide use in the 1950s, and the bird was on the federally endangered species list from 1970 to 1999. The falcon has found a safe home in the NRGPP thanks to "hacking" — the relocation of young falcons from bridge nests in surrounding states to areas in the park where the nestlings can grow and learn to fly with the least amount of human interaction. Nestlings from bridge nests are good candidates for relocation due to the risks of nesting young birds who can't fly over open water and due to collisions with motor vehicles. Hack nests at the New are partially enclosed cage-like structures on steep cliffs. The hack nests keep the nestlings safe from predators, while prey is dropped into the nest through a tube so that there is no association of food with humans. Nestlings stay in the hack nest, until they can fly —"fledge" — and develop their own hunting skills.

## Three Rivers Avian Center

The Three Rivers Avian Center on Brooks Mountain Road near Sandstone is a bird-lover's nonprofit agency that rehabilitates non-game and endangered birds. They provide emergency veterinarian care and release birds back into the wild once they return to health. Additionally, their programs help support scientific research about birds of the New River Gorge — barred owls, broad-winged hawks, redtail hawks, and others. Check their events calendar for the latest information about their Public Tour dates. Check their website at **www.tracwv.org**.

📷 TRAC

## Fish

The New River Gorge is home to multiple types of fish — rock, striped, smallmouth, and largemouth bass, as well as catfish, walleye, trout, crappie, bluegill, and carp. For your best chances of catching some of the many species of fish found swimming in the New River waterways, visit during fall or spring. Plan your fishing trips for either the early morning or late in the day to maximize the chance of luring a hungry fish. If you're specifically looking for trout, try Dunloup Creek near Glen Jean, Meadow Creek in Summers County, or the Gauley River in Fayette County. For catch-and-release bass fishing, try the 12-mile stretch of the New River between Sandstone and Grandview Sandbar.

# REGIONAL HISTORY

**Human activity in** the New River Gorge region has a long history dating from prehistoric times. Native Americans of many cultures and tribes hunted, fished, and farmed here, long before the first White settlers arrived. Railroads and coal mining left a huge impact on the region, not just on the physical landscape but in the diverse people these industries brought. In the past few decades, a thriving recreation and tourism industry has grown up around the rivers and hills of the gorge.

The history of the original people who called this region home is largely unknown. Archaeologists know that people lived in the New River region for 14,000 to 20,000 years before White settlers arrived. The oldest known are referred to as the Clovis people.

The earliest Clovis artifact discovered in the lower New River region is a spearpoint that has been dated to between 13,050 and 12,750 years ago. At that time, glaciers covered much of Ohio and Pennsylvania and the New River Gorge region was boreal forest that looked much like northern Canada or Alaska looks today. The Clovis people hunted BIG game: the now-extinct mastodon, as well as bison and caribou.

Between 12,000 and 10,000 years ago conditions began to warm, the glaciers retreated, and a deciduous forest gradually replaced the spruces and firs, bringing with it most of the current animal and plant species seen in the New River Gorge today. Little is known about how the Clovis people adapted to these changes, or if and when one group was replaced by others. We do know that the so-called Archaic period — 10,000 to 3000 years ago — was a time of innovation. Many different styles of notched and stemmed spearpoints appeared. There is evidence that people hunted deer, bear, small game, fish, and foraged for nuts and berries. Gourd and squash cultivation began around 6000 years ago, followed by cultivation of marsh elder, maygrass, sunflower, and other seed crops. Hunting tools continued to evolve, with the appearance of triangular and small notched points about 1300 years ago, heralding the arrival of the bow and arrow.

John Henry.

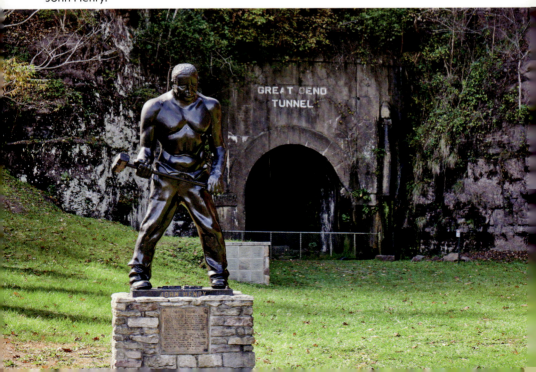

# Face in the Rock

## MONA LISA IN THE MOUNTAINS

This interesting art piece that's been described as the "Mona Lisa of the Mountains" is carved into a piece of stone at an obscure location near the rim of the New River Gorge: a life-size face, partly covered with moss thanks to decades of exposure to the elements. Local lore suggests the artist of this strange carving was a coal miner during the 1950s, although his reasons for carving the stone remain unclear.

To try to find the stone, head north on US 19 from Canyon Rim Visitor Center and turn onto Edmond/Lansing Road. Go 0.4 miles and turn right onto Fayette Station Road, drive 0.6 miles to a wide spot on the left with an info board. Go down the hill on the trail until the area opens up, go about 100 yards, cross the creek and it's on the left. You might have to search around a bit!

During the Woodland Period, 3000 to 900 years ago, residents of the New River region began making pottery for cooking and storage. The natural resources of the lush woodlands of West Virginia defined the Woodland culture. The people were hunters, gatherers, farmers, fishers, trappers, basket weavers, potters, and toolmakers. They roamed widely throughout the region to trade goods, traveling through the forest on foot, and on waterways via birch-bark canoe. In winter they used sleds. They married people from other tribes and regions and performed a variety of ceremonies.

One interesting development during the Woodland Period was the building of large earthen and stone mounds. These appear to have been burial structures for higher-status individuals and families, containing valuable objects including pottery, decorative stones, and clay pipes. Quite a few of these mounds are still visible today — the Criel Mound in Charleston is one nearby example you can visit. The eventual fate of the mound-building people is not known.

Between 900 and 500 years ago, during the so-called Late Prehistoric period, new developments included permanent agriculture in larger communities along waterways, a denser concentration of populations, and field crops including corn and beans. Arrow points continued to evolve, and there is evidence of increased social complexity as well as conflict and warfare.

The Buck Garden people lived throughout the New River region at this time. Living in compact villages, they raised beans,

Regional History

# Mary Draper Ingles

In July 1755, during the French and Indian War, 23-year-old Mary Draper Ingles and her two sons were kidnapped by the Shawnee near Blacksburg, Virginia, and taken east, into modern day Ohio. A few months later, Mary escaped and made her way home in a harrowing journey immortalized in West Virginia lore as well as several more modern films. In 40 days (mostly in the company of an older Dutch woman who tried several times late in the ordeal to kill her), Mary walked 500 miles, along waterways and through the New River Gorge, before arriving at a friend's house as winter was setting in. You can hike along the top of the north rim of the Gorge along the Endless Wall Trail or along the south river bank from Cunard to Thurmond and wonder what the New would have been like with no trails. Mary only carried a blanket, a tomahawk and knife, on her remarkable journey. One son also survived captivity. To see where Mary Ingles entered the New River Gorge, go to Cotton Hill, on Highway 16 north of Fayetteville, where the road crosses the New River, where a short trail follows an old service road up the river to just below the Hawks Nest Dam.

foraged roots, greens, berries, and ramps, fished, and hunted game. Archaeological evidence suggest they used rocks to make fishing jetties and game-herding fences. The most notable rock fences can be found in Mount Carbon, on the south side of the Kanawha River along US 60 between Gauley Bridge and Montgomery. An historical marker notes the archaeological site, which features rock walls, cairns, and small mounds. If you stand atop the cliff edge and look out over the overlapping tree-covered hills and ridge lines, it's possible to imagine the people living here, working with the land and the seasons.

For the last few hundred years before the first Whites appeared in the New, a cooling climate (often called the Little Ice Age) saw significant migration from southern Ohio, with new peoples settling along the bottomlands of the New River.

The Protohistoric period — 1492 until about 1650 — refers to the final period before Whites began keeping written historical records that documented parts of Native American culture. Archaeological excavations have recovered goods such as glass beads that indicate that the native peoples had some contact with White traders and pioneers. Without reliable written records, it is still uncertain how these Native Americans known to archaeologists were connected to historic local tribes such as the Cherokee and Shawnee.

During this final time before White settlers completely upended Native American life, archaeologists think that two similar but separate peoples inhabited the gorge: the Moneton and the Tutelo. Their language is thought to have been a Siouan in origin, sharing its root with early Great Plains tribes. Experts at foraging, horticulture, and food preservation, the Moneton and Tutelo harvested strawberries, chestnuts, watercress, wild grape, as well as edible herbs, greens, and roots. They cultivated corns, beans, and squash, and gathered wild rice, wild greens, seeds, berries, nuts, and fruit. Meat and fish were often dried, salted, and smoked for preservation. Foods were stored in clay pots and often buried to keep them cool and safe from pests.

Housing was in two forms, small wigwams and bigger longhouses, both framed with saplings and covered with bark or woven reeds. Related families lived together in longhouses, sharing food, childcare, and chores. Wigwams were probably single-family homes. Both wigwams and longhouses were only semi-permanent. When soil fertility declined, whole communities frequently moved short distances to re-establish their crops in new soil.

Ceremonies were held throughout the year, celebrating the cycle of the moon, the growth and harvest of crops, the change of seasons, as well as community and family. Dancing, singing, chanting, fasting, and ceremonial baths were all performed during ceremonies, and people smoked the peace pipe made of clay and filled with herbal blends that did not contain nicotine or have psychotropic qualities. It is believed that the Moneton and Tutelo merged with the Saponi tribe in the late 1600s.

## WHITES ARRIVE

In the 1670s, an expedition from the British Virginia Colony explored as far into the region as Kanawha Falls near present-day Gauley Bridge. These were the first Whites to see the area, along with French missionaries, who in the late 1600s reported several thousand Native Americans living in the area that is now central West Virginia. As the Whites began to populate the East Coast, they introduced new foods, new animals, new technologies, and new ways of life — as well as massive social upheaval and widespread conflict. Although the Treaty of Albany, signed in 1722, designated the Blue Ridge Mountains as the western boundary of White settlement, that and other agreements were quickly eclipsed and Whites would eventually almost completely replace the original natives of the land.

The 1671 Robert Fallam and Thomas Batts expedition recorded the first contact with native peoples living in the New River area, the Totero. Initial interactions were friendly and many native people adopted the customs and practices of White culture. Religion and language were impacted significantly by interactions and natives began practicing Christianity and speaking English. Native pottery and ceramics remained in high demand, but were heavily influenced by European styles and uses. While the people still fished, hunted, and raised crops, they began growing cotton and raised livestock to sell for cash. Natives adopted new housing styles with wood planks replacing bark and woven mats for wall and roofing coverage. Traded forged-iron tools replaced chipped stone.

## BATEAUX ON THE NEW

In 1812, John Marshall set out on an expedition to discover a navigable waterway from Virginia to the Ohio River Valley. Paddling 60-foot, flat bottomed boats known as bateaux, the expedition moved slowly, as the large boats had great difficulty navigating the rocky river and often got hung up in shallow water. The expedition ended at the confluence with the Gauley (now Gauley Bridge) and is the first recorded boat trip through the New River Gorge.

When Virginia voted to secede from the Union at the start of the Civil War, most of the population of present-day West Virginia opposed the secession. In all, 11 southern states severed ties with the Union and declared themselves the Confederate States of America. Twenty-one northern states retained the structure and title of the United States. A battle between Union and Confederate soldiers occurred in September 1862 in Fayetteville. There is a historical sign on the Court House lawn marking the spot, and the battle helped the Confederate forces gain control of the Kanawha Valley. Confederates controlled Fayetteville for just a month, before going east to defend Virginia. West Virginia (originally named Kanawha) gained official statehood in the throes of the Civil War, when on June 20th, 1863, the U.S. government recognized it as the 35th state.

## BLACK AMERICAN HISTORY

Before the Civil War, there were approximately 20,000 slaves, 3600 slave owners, and 2800 freedmen living in what is now West Virginia. Enslaved African Americans did a broad range of work — in agriculture, mining, industry, transportation, and commerce.

Although the original Africans came from different regions with very different, sometimes warring cultures, the institution of slavery brought the Black community together, resulting in vibrant folklore, music, and religion — a vital community and culture supporting human dignity in the face of great adversity. From caring for enslaver's families and raising their children, to their language, art, music, cuisine, and African traditions, Black Americans have exerted a

# The African American Heritage Tour

A self-guided driving tour and smartphone app, the African American Heritage Tour was developed by Park Service and partners to allow visitors to explore the region while learning the history and the stories of black coal miners, railroad workers, and other community members that shaped the New River Gorge region. The auto tour comprises 17 historic sites in Summers, Raleigh, Fayette, and Nicholas counties to learn about the history and experiences of the region's African Americans. The tour is available through the NPS app for NRGNPP, or stop by a park visitor center more info.

In 1872, an anthology "Slave Songs of the United States" was published. Compiled by abolitionists Charles Pickard Ware, Lucy McKim Garrison, and William Francis Allen, it was the first published compilation of African American music and documents 136 songs.

The greater New River area was home to several significant figures in Black history. The most prominent African American speaker of his time, Booker T. Washington hailed from just downstream of the New River Gorge. At age 9, Washington started as a (paid) worker in the Malden salt mine along the Kanawha River near Charleston. In 1872, at 16, he walked 500 miles to begin studies at the Hampton Institute, a school for formerly enslaved people in southeastern Virginia. There he excelled, and soon became an advocate for education and entrepreneurship for Black Americans. He was also an educator, author, orator, and adviser to several U.S. presidents. There is a Booker T. Washington monument on the grounds of the state capitol complex in Charleston.

A contemporary of Booker T. Washington, in 1894 George Washington Carver became the first African American to earn a Bachelor of Science degree, from the Iowa State Agricultural School (now Iowa State University). Carver's research on soil chemistry led to his concept of crop rotation. Discovering that growing only cotton depleted soil nutrients, he recommended alternating with nitrogen-fixing crops such as sweet potatoes, peanuts, and soybeans to restore soil nutrients. This rotational method resulted in a dramatic yield increase in cotton crops.

Named after these two Black luminaries, Camp Washington-Carver in Fayette County is just a short drive from the New River Gorge near Babcock State Park. Constructed by the Civilian Conservation Corps, it opened in 1942 as the first 4-H Camp in the country for African-American youth. Today Camp Washington-Carver hosts the Heritage Arts Camp, the Appalachian String Band Festival, and is home to the largest log structure of its kind in the world, the Great Chestnut Lodge.

No mention of Black history in West Virginia would be complete without acknowledging Carter G. Woodson, often called the Father of Black History. Woodson worked in the Kaymoor and Nuttallburg coal mines in the heart of the gorge, and when his fellow workers

profound influence, shaping and creating Appalachian culture. Music was integral to daily life; songs were sung in fields and railroad work sites.

African traditions include the distinctive call-and-response heard today in many churches. The Christian gospels were ripe with material for remixing into spiritual preaching and music about deliverance, salvation, hope, and resistance. Shouts, stomps, clapping, and sorrow songs also came from Black roots. African proverbs taught valuable lessons to Black children — tales of cunning tricksters, in the form of tortoises, spiders, or rabbits, defeating more powerful enemies through patience, wit, and guile.

Hawks Nest Tunnel. 📷 NPS

shared tales, Woodson carefully documented their stories, struggles, and experiences. He saved his miner's pay for his education to become a teacher in the New River Gorge mining town of Winona.

Like the immigrant White coal workers who would soon join them, the early Black workers did the hardest work with the lowest pay. Installing the heavy ties and rails for the steep, winding rail lines in the mountains of Appalachia was a never-ending task, and African-American workers known as "gandy dancers" secured the wood and steel with hefty spikes, the driving of which was coordinated by rhythmic songs old and new. There was no glory in those oppressive days, only grit and pride, but one thing is for sure: the work of thousands of Black Americans was an essential ingredient in West Virginia's industrial rise.

## THE RAILROADS

The New River Gorge region's industrial ascendancy was based on two developments that were intimately entwined: the opening of the railroads and coal mining. The gorge was full of valuable coal, but it was worthless if it couldn't be brought to market by the thousands of tons. Railroads could make that happen, but they would require huge and immediate profits to justify the infrastructure investment. It was a match made in heaven — or hell?

Three main railroad companies were active in West Virginia: the Virginian, the Norfolk & Western, and most relevant to the NRGNPP region, the Chesapeake & Ohio Railway that focused on routes along the New and Kanawha rivers.

The C&O Railway wanted to lay track right along riverbanks, and bought the right of way through the New River Gorge from local coal company owner Martin Blume. Of the project's six sections, two were along the New River: a 36-mile section from the Greenbrier River, near Hinton to the Great Bend below Grandview and a 28-mile section from Great Bend to Gauley Bridge.

Building a railroad through the gorge was more difficult than the engineers expected. From the outset, workers faced dangerous conditions and construction problems. The

# Old Thurmond

The largest landowners in southern West Virginia were from Ohio. These included Thomas Gaylord McKell and his wife Jean Dun McKell, who were gifted lands near Dunloup in 1880. McKell instantly saw the opportunity for wealth in the timber on the land and the coal beneath it and bought more land. McKell chose Glen Jean, near present-day Oak Hill, to build a town. McKell built a hotel and bank, mercantile operations, and rental properties. The National Park Service now owns the bank — it's the beautiful sandstone building across from the NPS Headquarters in Glen Jean. To transport his coal and timber to market, McKell negotiated with the C&O railroad to construct a line seven miles up Dunloup Creek — route of the present-day Thurmond Road — on the condition to build a coal plant that would be able to process 1000 tons of coal a day. He built a bridge over the New River to connect his holdings in Glen Jean and Dun Glen with the C&O mainline, and leased land to mine operator Justus Collins, who formed the Collins Colliery Company. Collins opened two mines behind town, when the C&O completed the Dunloup Branch. In 1893, the second-biggest mining operation in New River coalfields began production.

The connection point of the Dunloup branch and the C&O main line was the town of Thurmond, a New River landmark to this day. In 1873, Captain W. D. Thurmond had acquired 73 acres along the New River and the C&O railroad. In those days his property, in the heart of the New River Gorge, was the perfect location for a town. The timber and coal industries were growing, and so was the town. Freight wasn't the railroad's only source of income; passengers quickly became a viable business concern. A post office opened in 1888, and in its heyday, Thurmond had a movie theater, restaurants, a jewelry store, dry-goods stores, two hotels, and many business offices. By 1910 the railroad carried 75,000 passengers through Thurmond.

McKell opened the 100 room Dun Glen hotel in 1901; among the many memorable events in its short heyday, the hotel holds the record for the longest poker game in history — 14 years.

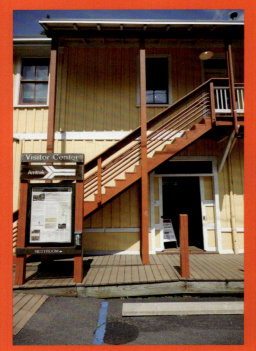

The Dun Glen was set afire by arsonists in the 1930s, marking the beginning of the end of the town of Thurmond as a cultural center. Today the site is an historical curiosity, and it's fun to walk or bike around town, or even ride the train through the Gorge. More adventurous folks can participate in the Captain Thurmond's Triathlon, that lets you kayak, mountain bike, and run from Thurmond to Fayetteville.

track ran through steep sandstone cliffs that required significant excavations. Landslides, drownings, and silicosis (black lung disease) from the tunnelling work injured and killed workers, further slowing construction. The railroad finally opened to commercial traffic in March 1873.

The C&O rail line opened up the New River Gorge to massive resource extraction, and in fall of 1873 the first coal shipped out of the gorge, from the Quinnimont mine below Grandview. The railroad began to expand rapidly. By the late 1880s, branch lines had been constructed in most of the gorge's larger tributaries, opening up virgin coalfields as well as timber. The Sewell coal seam along Keeney Creek near the town of Winona started producing in 1890. Thurmond and Quinnimont digs were served by the Laurel Creek and Loop Creek branches. Mines in Clifftop were served by the Mann's Creek Branch, while the Sewell Valley Railroad transported lumber to the large band mills in Honeydew, Nallen, and Rainelle along the Meadow River east of the park. Development by C&O's rival railroad companies led to the opening of coalfields farther south in the state, producing the boom towns of Oak Hill and Beckley. Coal production in West Virginia increased from 489,000 tons in 1869 to almost 90 million tons in 1917.

Small timber operations had been going on in the gorge for years, but once the railroad branch lines were established, large-scale logging began. The coal company's demand for lumber for tipples, plant building, and miner housing was insatiable and quickly depleted local resources. Yellow poplar, black walnut, oak, chestnut, basswood, hemlock, beech, and hickory along the New, Gauley, and Kanawha Rivers were aggressively harvested. By the 1920s they would be nearly gone. Sawmills became a booming industry, with mill towns popping up throughout the gorge. As the timber was harvested, towns would flourish, only to collapse when the wood was gone. The scale of the logging operations is hard to imagine today. At one time, the Meadow River Lumber Company, at Rainelle, just east of the gorge, was the largest lumber and mill operation in the world.

## COAL

Located on the eastern flank of the Appalachian coal basin, the New River was home to 13 bituminous coalbeds, each at least 14 inches thick and approximately 300 million years old. Deeply buried in most of the region, these coalbeds were exposed in the deep canyon of the New River Gorge. The most abundant mineral resource in the region, bituminous coal is a low-sulfur, smokeless, high-quality coal whose low moisture and high carbon content make it ideal for generating electricity and producing steel. Early coal mining was negligible until the railroad made coal transport on a large scale possible. In 1871, John Nuttall and Joseph Beury began coal mining the Sewell seam in anticipation of completing the C&O railroad. Beury and Nuttall established the first large-scale operation in the gorge and shipped the first load of coal out of the Quinnimont mine in Laurel Creek. The Sewell, Beury, and Nuttallburg mines quickly opened, building small mining towns. These operations mined coal for either direct sale, or processed it for sale as coke (coal with most of the volatile impurities baked out of it) for industry.

Construction of the C&O lines brought thousands of workers into the area. Adding to the existing population of Native Americans, British & French, and Black Americans, the new state of West Virginia became home to Mexican, Chinese, Sottish, Irish, German, Italian, and Eastern European immigrants. This population boom would further diversify the foundation for the Appalachian culture of customs, art, food, and music that endures today. Yet the struggle, strife, and conflict that started when the first colonists came to America would continue for many decades, springing from the dangers and hardships of railroad and mining work, and the ruthlessness of

Kaymoor miners, 1922. 📷 NPS

Kaymoor haulage. 📷 NPS

many company owners. Nevertheless, along the way, workers would build families and vibrant communities that fused and blended truly global traditions, cultures, and heritage. At the close of the 1800s, there were more than a dozen mining towns in the gorge between Fayette Station and Thurmond.

Coal extraction drastically affected the once-pristine natural environment of the New River Gorge. All flat land was used for the structures required for coal and coke-processing facilities. Whether level or sloped, land around the mines was developed for housing, service, or recreational buildings — always very tightly spaced to maximize the utility of the gorge's limited terrain. Conditions were harsh, communities were crowded, and coal dust was inescapable.

The mining towns were company towns — planned, company-controlled, and often very isolated. Miners and their families were entirely dependent on the coal companies for all of life's necessities — stores, schools, theaters, churches, doctors. Instead of receiving cash they could spend anywhere, or save for a better life, miners were paid in scrip, which could be traded for company goods and services, at notoriously high prices. Miners and their families were captive to the company store and quickly accumulated inescapable debt.

Italians were the most numerous immigrant group in the area. They arrived to build the railroads and stayed on as miners. Many were skilled masons who supervised the building of coke ovens and other stone structures in the gorge. The second largest group was Austro-Hungarian, who worked almost exclusively as pick-miners. African Americans, Germans, Croatians, Slavs, and others worked in the mines. "Native" Whites moved into supervisory or day-wage positions. As large numbers of immigrants populated the area, native Whites began to move out, seeking higher wages in unionized mines elsewhere. The mining companies advertised equal pay for all workers, which gave immigrants and African Americans a sense of equity, but the companies did not foster equity and equality. Too much esprit de corps among the workers could unite them against the company. Instead, when companies built housing they built residences in groups for different ethnicities. The mines in southern West Virginia were run in a particularly ruthless fashion, with the companies hiring private detective agencies to surveil workers and break up meetings that could lead to unions forming. Such mistreatment and exploitation of workers would soon lead to deadly clashes.

## THE MINING WARS

This industrial success story had a dark underbelly. Miners were exposed to coal dust and toxic fumes and metals, putting them at risk for silicosis and pneumoconiosis, commonly referred to as black lung. Mine collapses were common, killing many miners. Between 1890 and 1912, West Virginia mines had the highest death rates in the United States: West Virginia miners faced higher death rates than American soldiers fighting in Europe during World War I.

As individuals, miners were powerless against the powerful coal companies, but as a group they could effect change. The first miner's strike in West Virginia was at Hawk's Nest, at the downstream end of the gorge, in 1880. The United Mine Workers of America (UMWA) formed in 1890, managing many

# The Battle of Blair Mountain

The 1920 "Matewan Massacre" was another dark spot in West Virginia history, and the catalyst that led to a march on Logan County (just west of the gorge) and the so-called Battle of Blair Mountain — perhaps the most significant armed labor uprising in United States history. In Matewan, southwest of the gorge region on the Kentucky border, a deadly shootout occurred on May 19, 1920 between Baldwin–Felts company-hired guards, the town sheriff and mayor, and local miners. Striking miners who had been evicted from their coal-company homes were living in a nearby tent camp. Mine guards attempted to forcibly remove them, despite lacking any legal authority.

After investigating the unlawful evictions, Sheriff Hatfield and Mayor Testerman had a heated verbal altercation with the guards, which turned into a violent shootout that left the mayor, seven guards, and two townspeople dead. Hostilities, strikes, and marches continued, and the next year Sheriff Hatfield was gunned down by company-hired mine guards, becoming an enduring union hero.

Hatfield's death set off a series of marches, originally urged on by the UMWA. The goal was to force coal companies to accept the union. On August 24, 5000 armed miners began marching from Marmet to Mingo County and the base of Blair Mountain. Troops established fortifications atop a ridge on Blair Mountain under the direction of Logan County Sheriff Don Chafin. Shooting began on August 27 and quickly escalated into a battle. Chafin authorized deputized townspeople to drop homemade pipe bombs on the miners. Both sides exchanged gunfire, killing 12 miners and four townspeople on the side of the coal companies. The battle is the closest thing to a class war that the United States has experienced, with over 100 people killed, the most prominent armed uprising on U.S. soil outside of the Civil War. Miners surrendered when President Warren G. Harding deployed federal troops on September 2, 1921. Rather than achieving the miners' goals, the fighting nearly destroyed the UMWA. Membership in West Virginia dropped to less than 1000. It wasn't until President Franklin Roosevelt's New Deal, in 1933, that miners and the UMWA were again allowed to organize in West Virginia.

strikes at coal mines farther north, but at first union membership in the New River Gorge region remained low. At the time, the UMWA's only negotiating tactic was to pull miners off the site and shut down the mines — difficult or impossible for miners living in remote company towns deep in the gorge. Mining company owners aggressively resisted efforts to organize and strike, hiring armed guards from private detective agencies to prevent uprisings.

Nevertheless, oppressive conditions and poverty led to increasing resentment and resistance among miners. Numerous small strikes ensued. Then in April 1912 at Paint Creek in Kanawha County, miners walked off the job demanding better pay, the right to organize, and an end to the mine-guard system. This was a so-called wildcat strike, done without union assistance, and soon 7500 miners from Cabin Creek also joined. When mine "guards" (from the notorious Baldwin–Felts Detective Agency) forcibly evicted mining families from their homes, throwing their possessions on the ground, violence erupted. The Paint Creek-Cabin Creek Strike marked the beginning of the West Virginia Mine Wars. Siding with the mining companies, Governor William Glasscock declared martial law and deployed the National Guard. The strike lasted for over a year and by the end 12 miners and 13 company men were dead.

The coal industry flourished in the New until the Great Depression, when coal production declined sharply. Coal boomed again during World War II, but mines closed again afterward, with only a few smaller operations continuing to function. With the closing of the mines, people sought opportunities elsewhere, leaving ghost towns, and the abandoned mines and towns slowly decayed. Many of the mining buildings and tipples were torn down, while others collapsed or burned. A few small communities survived. Today, coal-mine sites and artifacts make up New River's most significant and abundant cultural resources.

## OUTDOOR RECREATION

After the decline of mining, the area around the Gorge was quiet for decades. The smoky air cleared and forests grew back, but young folks moved away due to lack of opportunities. That started to change in the 1960s, as outdoor recreation became "a thing." The rivers, cliffs, and forests of the New were rediscovered.

The dramatic, Grand-Canyon scale whitewater rapids of the New River were the first features to put the region back on the map. The Dragon family — Jon, Tom, Chris, and Melanie — started rafting and taking friends down the New in 1968. The entrepreneurial grit and adventurous spirit these folks brought to the New changed everything. They were a self-taught crew, but quickly learned how to read the water, bought a few surplus rafts and a couple of pick-up trucks, and started the region's first rafting company, Wildwater Unlimited Expeditions.

## Aerial Tour with Wild Blue

If you really want to see the New, book an aerial tour with **Wild Blue Adventure Company**. We guarantee it's a once-in-a-lifetime experience. The company is owned by longtime locals Bill Chouinard, his wife Ashley, and their family — you'll be in good hands! While taking in the majesty of the gorge you'll fly in a 1943 Boeing Stearman, an open-cockpit fully restored, museum-quality, WWII-era biplane. For the daring, you can add aerobatics as an option to your tour — experience barrel rolls, hammerheads, cravats, and s-turns. Reservations are highly recommended in order to guarantee your flight at your desired date and time. Note that flights may be re-scheduled in case of bad weather. www.wildblueadventurecompany.com

The Dragons mapped the river and named many of the rapids. Many were named during the first trips down the river. Imagine how exciting it would be to navigate those unknown waters — especially when the rapids ended up with names like Surprise, Double Z, and Greyhound Bus Stopper. Yes, there are rapids down there that will seriously surprise you, others that make you zig-zag back and forth across the river, and there are "holes" on the New River big enough to "stop a Greyhound bus."

At that time there was no National Park, no river rangers, and no laws or safety requirements. (Within a decade, the West Virginia Department of Natural Resources began regulating rafting on the New.) In the first few years, Wildwater Unlimited Expeditions had more guides than guests, but the Dragons' vision was less about money than it was about the experience. They offered a two-day trip that started at Prince, camped overnight at Thurmond, and spent the second day on the lower New, taking out below Fayette Station. The Gauley is the other big commercially run river in the NRGNPP region; the Dragons' first commercial trip down that one was in 1971.

Soon after Wildwater Unlimited Expeditions started rafting tours, Mountain River Tours (MRT, and locally called "Mert") opened. MRT is credited with really opening up rafting access on the Gauley. At the time of the early trips, there was no mid-point access to the very long stretch of challenging river, meaning folks would have to raft the entire 26 miles of river from the Summersville Dam to the town of Swiss — definitely not feasible for a commercial day trip. MRT purchased land at Woods Ferry, which made it possible to raft either the upper or lower section, which made commercial trips more viable.

Completed on October 22, 1977, the New River Gorge Bridge was a game changer, not just for whitewater rafting, but the area in general. Before the bridge was completed one had to drive down into the gorge, cross the river on a little bridge — the easiest route being Fayette Station Road — and drive up a steep, winding road on the other side. On a good day it would take 40 minutes, but if you got behind a big truck or a driver who didn't know how to navigate the hairpin turns it could take much longer. Our dad reminisces that as a young man he'd attend a church social or community dance, and if you met someone you liked, the first thing you'd ask was what side of the gorge they lived on. If you weren't both from the same side, there was no point getting to know them as you'd probably never see them again.

Regional History 51

The bridge changed the way the whitewater rafting trips could be offered. In order to drop and pick-up rafting guests, the companies previously had to drive from their base camps to Thurmond (the put-in), then drive to below Hawk's Nest Pool (the take-out). The long commutes and spotty river access made high-volume commercial rafting nearly impossible: guests would have to be committed to spending 10 hours on the river, finishing up with paddling out several miles of flat water.

In the late the 1970s, with the bridge opening up access and rafting steadily growing, the National Park Service recognized the abundance of scenic and recreational opportunities in the area, as well as its outstanding cultural and natural history. This needed to be preserved! In 1978, President Jimmy Carter signed legislation that established the New River Gorge National River.

During the peak rafting years in the 1990s, approximately 225,000 people rafted each season. Rafting companies had to accommodate staff and guests who traveled from out of state, so they built campgrounds and even restaurants. Since then, the numbers have slowly declined. Smaller rafting companies closed their doors while the others began merging. Seeking to add more experiences to attract guests, companies added playgrounds, ropes courses, ziplines and canopy tours, water parks, pools, horseback riding, trails, and ... well you get the idea, pretty much something for everyone. It's completely possible now to stay at Adventures on the Gorge, ACE, or New & Gauley River Adventures and have the time of your life ... without even going rafting!

A new local culture grew up around whitewater rafting, adding a new layer to the old coal-mining and logging heritage. As whitewater recreation was taking off, rock climbers discovered the cliffs along the rim of the gorge, which happened to be some of the best climbing rock in the East. Kenny Parker was 19 years old Gorge in 1983 when he first climbed in the New River. He recalls, "We'd heard about this mythical, vast, unexplored climbing area. So, we stopped at the New and ended up getting lost in the woods, bushwhacking everywhere looking for cliffs." At the time there were few trails and very few other climbers, but miles of cliff lay hiding in the Appalachian jungles waiting to be discovered. By 1987 there were 375 documented routes, by 1996 there were over 1500, and the current guidebook, *New River Rock* by Michael Williams, details over 3000 routes at dozens of different cliffs from the gorge proper to Summersville Lake.

By the end of the 1990s, the New River Gorge area was known to boaters and climbers around the country and the globe. Mountain-biking trails were developed, running and adventure races filled out the calendar, while restaurants, breweries, and Airbnbs made the small towns vibrant, fun recreational communities. It's fair to call the New an outdoor recreational mecca — enough to make you want to live there. Which is exactly what has happened. Many who were exposed to the area on a rafting, hiking, or climbing trip are now residents.

In 1994 when Maura and Gene Kistler opened Water Stone Outdoors (known as Blue Ridge Outdoors at the time) and formed the New River Gorge Alliance of Climbers (NRAC) in Fayetteville with Kenny Parker, they saw a need and an opportunity in the community to get more people outdoors and connecting to nature, to create a community of participation around conservation. The idea, says Maura, was simple: "If people love the outdoors, they'll be invested in protecting it. If the outdoor community isn't fully invested in saving the planet, then who is?" At the time they didn't know it, but they built the foundations not only of recreation and conservation in the area, but also of the "coolest small town" of Fayetteville.

As of 2022 Water Stone has new proprietors; Holly Fussell, her husband Chris, and their two children heeded the call to make the mountains of the New River Gorge home and work. Holly and family are equal-opportunity recreation enthusiasts; along with climbing, they enjoy mountain biking, trail running, hiking, lake swimming, stand-up paddle boarding, and whitewater paddling. Nothing makes them happier than exposing others to the beauty and challenges of the NRG, and seeing the awakening and empowerment that so often follows.

Water Stone remains an epicenter of outdoor adventure sports to this day. If that's your thing (and even if it isn't), check out the shop, located right across from the Fayetteville Courthouse. In a world full of too many big-box stores, it's as "cool" as you get!

# Welcome to the 'Ville

Fayetteville is the heart and soul of the New River Gorge region and home to Canyon Rim Visitor Center and the New River Gorge Bridge. While a lot of history is found in Fayetteville, most people visiting come for modern-day fun and adventures and all the great restaurants. With a town full of friendly locals ready to share the best ways to experience their town, there are tons of things you don't want to miss when visiting Fayetteville. Explore and enjoy!

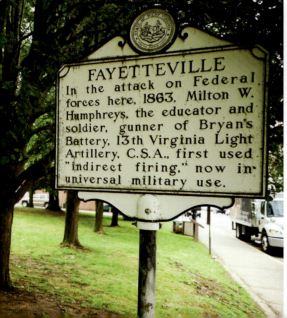

# VISITING

# PLAYING IN THE PARK

## PLANNING AND PACKING

The New is a multi-sport destination. With so many outdoor activities to explore, good planning and packing is key. Smart choices about where to stay will help you do your day's activities without having to drive to the opposite end of the park (unless you want to). If you're most interested in the area around the Sandstone Visitor Center, for example, stay in Hinton, which will also put you close to the John Henry Museum and Three Rivers Avian Center. Hinton also has a train station. To explore the areas around Canyon Rim Visitor Center and the New River Gorge Bridge, on the other hand, stay in or near Fayetteville, which is closest to the best hiking and biking trails on the rim of the gorge, all the rock-climbing areas, and old mine ruins at Kaymoor and Nuttallburg.

## About the Weather

There's a local expression here: "If you don't like the weather, wait 15 minutes." In other words, have clothing and gear for changing conditions. The mountains here are known for weather that can turn on a dime, so don't get caught unprepared in a "sudden downpour that appeared out of nowhere." Those are normal.

## What to Wear

When venturing away from your car, bring well-chosen layers you can easily add or remove as conditions (and you) get warmer, colder, or wetter. You'll want a lightweight

rain jacket for the spring and summer months, even if the forecast calls for clear skies. Synthetic or wool layers dry faster and keep you warmer when wet than cotton — which could save the day on a late-season hike or a chilly rafting outing. Good hiking shoes (or hiking sandals) will pay dividends on the often-rough trails of the park; street shoes and flip-flops make you work harder and may even be hazardous on certain trails. If you don't have any real outdoor clothing, make a stop at Water Stone Outdoors in Fayetteville, one of the best outdoor specialty shops anywhere. It's a local landmark.

If you specialize in certain activities and have your own gear — bring it! If you have room, that is. To do all the possible outdoor activities in the park you would need ropes and technical climbing gear, a flatwater craft, a whitewater craft, PFDs and helmets, car-camping gear, backpacking gear, road and mountain bikes, fishing gear — maybe even a BASE-jumping outfit! Obviously, you'll need to prioritize. Fortunately, there are also plenty of places to rent gear or do guided activities like rafting or climbing where gear is supplied.

## OUTDOOR RECREATION

Now that you're wise about the layout of the park, what to bring, and how to plan, let's get to the outdoor adventures that await. For climbers, hikers, or paddlers, there are dedicated books for each of those activities, so only a sampling of the options is given here. With over 70,000 acres and multiple access points, it doesn't matter your fitness level or ability — there is truly something for everyone at the New.

## Spotty Service

Cell coverage is fickle in the region, especially in the gorge, so don't rely solely on your cell phone for navigation. Download maps of the areas you plan to visit so that you can access them even when out of signal range. Alternately, pick up a copy of the excellent NPS map at one of the visitor centers.

# Pet Etiquette and Leash Laws

Dogs are welcome on any of the trails in the NRGNPP. Dogs are not permitted in the public ranger programs, however, so plan accordingly. For all things pets, visit www.nps.gov/neri/planyourvisit/pets.htm

Even though your dog is allowed on the trails, you'll still need to abide by some rules:

- Your dog must be on leash. The maximum allowed leash length is six feet.
- Harmful bacteria may be present in streams, so you may want to bring enough water on hikes and outings for Rufus as well as yourself. A lightweight collapsible bowl is helpful.
- Pack a little more food than normal for your pup. Chances are they'll be working harder than they're used to and burning more calories. Bringing the same food and treats they eat at home can help them feel more comfortable.
- Pets need rest, and can easily overheat. If not lazy and sluggish, they'll be over excited; prevent them from exhausting themselves, and give them a few minutes to cool down every now and then. If your dog is especially prone to overheating, consider purchasing a cooling mat or collar.
- The park requests that owners always pick up after their pets on the trail. No one enjoys encountering pet waste while out in nature. Not only is it a nuisance, it spreads disease among the park's wild animals. Pack plenty of waste bags. Once you've bagged your pet's poop, pack it out; don't leave it alongside the trail, assuming a ranger or other hikers will deal with it. Double-bag it to protect your pack.
- Before bringing your dog into the NRGNPP, make sure they are up to date on their vaccinations, and flea and tick medication. Microchipping is a great idea. Likewise, if you haven't already, now's the perfect time to personalize Fluffy's collar with your phone number and address, lest she find a permanent home in West Virginia.

# SCENIC DRIVES

**Most visitors come** to the park by private vehicle. Most will tour around a bit in that vehicle, and — no surprise — the New River Gorge area is rich in scenic drives. If you or a family member has difficulty traversing foot trails, drives are the perfect way to see the park. These are also excellent motorcycle rides.

Nearly every access point to the New River requires leaving major roadways and heading down backroads that wind steeply into the gorge. From the Canyon Rim Visitor Center, the first question rangers often hear is, "How do we get to the river?" It's not far, via Fayette Station Road, but to go direct from the visitor center you have to get past one of the tightest, steepest switchbacks you'll ever see on a paved road. Locals call it "Stupid's Corner," a reference to those who have left their signature dent in the guardrail trying to make the turn with a large vehicle, only to limp back to safety before they're even in the gorge. Word to the wise: unless you're confident and your vehicle has a good turning radius, go back out to the highway, head north, then take the next right toward Lansing, a much easier approach to Fayette Station Road.

Before you take the family car out for a spin on a bright, gorgeous afternoon, don't forget to grab a map, fill the tank, and pack plenty of water and snacks for yourself and the kiddos. You're sure to find places you'll want to explore, whether it's a ghost town or a hiking trail. Additionally, certain roads may be prone to washouts, so check with the rangers or locals for up-to-date road info.

Almost any backroad you drive in the region will be scenic, but here's a list of some of our favorites. Drive times do not include the many stops you'll likely make.

## COAL HERITAGE TRAIL

- The roads: Good two-lane highway, mostly winding and occasionally narrow.
- Distance: 125 miles, three hours driving time.

The National Coal Heritage Area includes 13 coal-producing counties in southern West Virginia. This drive, along a national scenic byway, will show you the beautiful mountain landscapes, small towns, architecture, and

industrial heritage of the coal fields of southern West Virginia. (While the area is rich in rail and coal history it also includes the wildly popular Hatfield and McCoy ATV trails. With over 700 miles of interconnected trails it's one of the largest off road trail systems in the United States.)

This drive tours the Coal Heritage area south of the park, starting at Bluefield, which is accessed from I-77 just north of the Virginia/West Virginia border, and ending at the Exhibition Coal Mine in Beckley. You can also start from Beckley and loop south. The drive takes you through many interesting small towns including Bluefield, Bramwell, Welch, Itmann, Mullens, Tams and Sophia.

From I-77 take exit 9 and follow Rt 460 west into Bluefield to catch Rt 52. In Bluefield you can stop by the still-active Bluefield Train Yard, which was instrumental in the development of the coal fields. You can also stop by Lotito City Park and hop a ride on the fully restored Ridge Runner No. 36 locomotive or walk through the park to stretch your legs.

Scenic Drives

From Bluefield, take 52N/Coal Heritage toward Bramwell; nine miles and about 20 minutes. Bramwell was the old millionaires' town and is home to the Coal Heritage Trail Interpretive Center, featuring exhibits of coal and train history and memorabilia of the heyday of the town. Most of the homes on the brick-lined streets of Bramwell are on the National Historic Register, while the bank of Bramwell, formed in 1889, was at one time thought to be the wealthiest bank per capita in the country. Great places to stop for a bite include the Corner Shop Diner, an old-fashioned ice cream parlor, and the Bramwell Outpost and Grill.

From Bramwell it's 18.3 miles on 52N/Coal Heritage to Kimball — about 25 minutes. A small town with a lot of history, Kimball is home to a memorial dedicated to WWI African American soldiers. For a unique souvenir, check out Coal Camp Creations on Main Street for figurines crafted out of local McDowell County coal.

From Kimball stay on Rt 52 for 7.2 miles to Welch. Welch has a fine historic district, the History of Our Mountains Museum, and is where detectives from the Baldwin-Felts Agency assassinated Matewan police chief Sid Hatfield and Ed Chambers during the West Virginia coal mine wars. Take a break at the Martha H Moore Riverfront Park, with a mural and river views, and for eats try the locally owned diners Sterling Drive-in and Spike's Dog House. During the summer, visitors can experience an outdoor production of the coal-mining wars, Terror of the Tug: meetmcdowell.com/terror-of-the-tug-10th-anniversary/

From Welch take WV 16N for 27 miles to Itmann — 40 minutes. Once a thriving coal camp, Itmann was built by coal baron I.T.

## Adena's Advice

Adena Joy, a New local for over 20 years, has made Fayetteville home for her and her three children. Owner of **Hills to Hills Shuttles and Tours**, Adena knows the ins and outs about driving around the New.

**Adena's Top Tips for a scenic drive:**
- The best thing you can bring on a scenic drive is a map and a sense of humor.
- Fill the gas tank, E stands for "empty," not "enough."
- When you drive through small towns, remember that they are communities: kids and pets live and play there.
- Driving on these narrow, winding roads is different than driving on highways or streets. Respect the posted speed limits, including the reduced speeds around turns.
- Stop, get out of your car, enjoy the view, take the pictures.
- Talk to folks. Introduce yourself and make friends.

Mann. You'll see old coal company houses along the road, as well as the old company store (not open, but makes for fun photos).

From Itman it's 3.5 miles on Rt 16 to Mullens, which has a really cool walking tour with over 20 historic buildings and sites including a hotel, bank, and Coca-Cola bottling plant.

From Mullens it's 19 more miles to Sophia on Rt 16 — about 35 minutes. Along the way you'll pass through Corrine, Helen, Amigo, Allen Junction, and Tams, very small communities with limited services. Tams was a large segregated mining town with two baptist churches and a catholic church, a large tipple, an aerial tramway, and a theater and store. In 1909, it was opened on Winding Creek by W.P. "Major" Tams' company, the Gulf Smokeless Coal Co. Major Tams was a larger-than-life character and was known as the last coal baron of the old era, he wrote an autobiography, "The Smokeless Coal Fields of West Virginia, and was interviewed in 1977 by Playboy Magazine. Only a few abandoned and desolate buildings remain. Sophia is home to Uptown Down a Vintage and Antique Shop, Daniel Vineyards and the restaurants Patty's, Main Street Café, and China One.

To get to the Beckley Exhibition Coal Mine from Sophia it's a little over 7 miles and takes about 15 minutes along WV 16N. You'll travel on WV16N/Robert C Byrd Drive 6.5 miles, then turn left on Ewart Ave. The Exhibition Mine is 0.7 miles down Ewart.

# RT 60/MIDLAND TRAIL

- The roads: Good two-lane highway, mostly winding occasionally narrow and steep.
- Distance: 60 miles and 1.5 hours.

Another National Scenic Byway, the Midland Trail (US 60) traverses nearly 200 miles of beautiful West Virginia scenery. Starting in Charleston, the Midland offers a scenic approach to the NRGNPP. You will follow the Kanawha River, first passing some of the state's important industrial sites such as the Chemours Chemical Plant in Belle and the Mammoth Coal Processing Plant in London. Soon the scenery turns more natural, with picturesque towns and nice river views. Just below Gauley Bridge, where the New and Gauley rivers flow together to form the Kanawha, you'll see Kanawha Falls, a good place for a stop, either at the public fishing area below the falls or the historic town of Glen Ferris just above. You'll then ascend a steep and winding stratch up Gauley Mountain, and up top you'll get eagle eye views of the New River at Hawks Nest. Experience the odd Mystery Hole before heading over to Canyon Rim Visitor Center for your first views of the New River Gorge Bridge.

From Charleston follow I-64 E/I-77S for about 11 miles to exit 96 to get on US60 E/Kanawha Blvd. You'll see signs for the Midland Trail. In about six miles you'll reach Belle. For

# MIDLAND TRAIL

such a small town, Belle has loads of history and fun things to do, with quaint riverside homes as well as the Samuel Shrewsbury House, a house and museum that accurately represents the early times of West Virginia. Fifteen miles later you can stop in Montgomery and hit the iconic Burger Carte, well known for their one-of-a-kind Mountain Mama, a burger topped with ramp aioli, smoked Gouda, bacon, onion, and fried green tomato. In another nine miles you'll come to a parking and fishing area below Kanawha Falls, a spacious and scenic area where you can get out and stretch your legs along the river. Just beyond is Glen Ferris, home to the 200-year-old Glen Ferris Inn, which served as a Union Army quartermaster's depot during the Civil War and is now a hotel and restaurant. Just past Glen Ferris is Gauley Bridge, where the New and the Gauley rivers join to form the Kanawha.

The next 12-mile section from Gauley Bridge to Hawks Nest gets steep and winding and takes at least 30 minutes to drive, a classic stretch of country road. Just outside of Gauley Bridge you'll pass Cathedral Falls on Cane Creek — at approximately 60 feet it is one of the highest waterfalls in West Virginia. The road soon ascends the flank of Gauley Mountain and follows the contours of the New River. Pull over at the overlooks for some inspiring views.

About 5 miles past Gauley Bridge, US 60 and US 16 will diverge, a spot known as Chimney Corner that is home to a restaurant and cool little gift store. Here you can choose to stay on US 60/Midland Trail and continue the tour, or take Rt 16 more directly to Fayetteville (also scenic).

Continuing on US 60, you'll pass Hawks Nest State Park with its gift shop, restaurant,

## NRG ATV

If your idea of a scenic drive is racing through the hills on an ATV, then check out the guided ATV adventure tours from New River ATV. They guide over 100 miles of trails, ranging from beginner to expert.
www.newriveratv.com/

Hawks Nest Overlook.

aerial tram, and overlook. There's enough to see and do at Hawks Nest to justify a night at the lodge. Throughout the summer Hawks Nest hosts a variety of fairs and festivals, so check their events calendar. New River Jet Boats offers family friendly rides here that are a fun way to experience the gorge and river.

From Hawks Nest it's about 30 more minutes to Canyon Rim. Pass the Mystery Hole, a kooky, iconic stop, then the town of Ansted with its well-preserved downtown. When you get to the intersection with US 19, turn right (south) toward Fayetteville and drive about five miles. The exit to Canyon Rim Visitor Center will be on your left and is well marked — you'll know you've gone too far if you drive across the bridge. Midland Trail does continue past US 19. If you wanted a longer drive you could continue on another 20 miles to Rainelle, then head south on Rt 20 and make your way to the Sandstone Visitor Center at the south end of the park — about 45 minutes from US 19.

## FAYETTE STATION ROAD

- The roads: Mostly one-way and one-lane, with steep drop-offs and switchbacks. Not suitable for RVs or trailers.
- Distance: 7.5 miles, 30 minutes.

This century-old route makes a deep dive into the gorge near Fayetteville, featuring a view of the New River Gorge Bridge from below, an up-close look at the river (including Fayette Station Rapid), plus various remnants of mining history. For this one you'll want a smaller vehicle, so if you're traveling by RV, swap it for a compact car for the day. You can also download a National Park Service audio tour of this drive: www.nps.gov/neri/learn/photosmultimedia/fayette-station-road-audio-tour.htm

From Canyon Rim Visitor Center turn right onto US 19. Go north for 0.2 miles, turn right onto Lansing-Edmond Rd, then go 0.2 miles and turn right onto Fayette Station Rd. From here it is 2.2 very slow miles to the bottom of the gorge; after about

## FAYETTE STATION AND NUTTALLBURG

three-quarters of a mile the road becomes one-way. At several points you will pass under the New River Gorge Bridge, with striking views of the steel girders. A half mile past the first under-bridge crossing you can escape the drive by turning right up Burma Rd, which will take you up to Ames Heights. Turn right and go 0.6 miles to get back to US 19. Beyond this, there's no turning back, and you will soon arrive at the picturesque and much smaller Tunney Hunsaker Bridge. You'll want to allow some extra time at the bottom for viewing the bridges and walking along the banks of the New. Depending on the time of day you may see rafts or kayakers running Fayette Station Rapid. To finish the drive, climb back out of the gorge by continuing along Fayette Station Road, 4.1 miles back to US 19, arriving directly across from Keller Ave, the back way into Fayetteville.

At Fayette Station.

Nuttallburg Coal Tipple.

## NUTTALLBURG MINE

- The roads: two-lane backroads, both paved and gravel. Some narrow, winding, and steep sections. Not suitable for RVs or trailers.
- Distance: 10 miles one-way, 30 minutes.

This is another Fayetteville-area drive that will take you down to the river. The lower part is very narrow — large vehicles or RVs not recommended! Lansing-Edmond Road passes by the Endless Wall trailheads and on to the quaint town of Winona; turn right here onto Keeney's Creek Rd and descend to the bottom of the gorge and the Nuttallburg Mine site. Nuttallburg has a couple of short trails (between half-a-mile and three miles long) and old mine ruins to explore along the banks of the New River.

From northbound US 19, just north of Canyon Rim Visitor Center, turn right (southeast) onto Lansing-Edmond Rd. Go six miles to Winona and turn right onto Keeney's Creek Road; the final four-mile section is steep and narrow and dead-ends at the Nuttallburg mine. If you plan to stay in Nuttallburg for any length of time, bring all your own water and snacks, as none are available on-site.

## Country Roads

Many roads in these parts are narrow, winding, and alternate between sun and deep shadow. Some can be intimidating to drive on! There's also a good chance you will come across cyclists, pedestrians, ATVs, slow-moving farm vehicles, chickens, dogs, and children. You need to be driving slow enough, and with enough attention and control, to react and respond to every road user. Expect turns to be sharp, so observe posted speed limits, which are often quite liberal! If you are from a tamer part of the country, you may not have seen this before: some paved roads in the area are only one lane. When another vehicle approaches you will be expected to share the road, dropping two wheels off the road onto the shoulder, ensuring that there is enough space between your vehicle and the one oncoming. If the oncoming driver is a local and mistakes you for one, they may not slow down much. Keep an eye out for branches, potholes, or ditches! The key thing to remember when traveling the backroads is to be alert, safe, and courteous to anyone you encounter.

## THURMOND ROAD

- The roads: narrow and winding in places; RVs, large vehicles, and trailers not recommended.
- Distance: 9.8 miles one-way, 25 minutes.

Start this drive near the New River Gorge National Park and Preserve's official headquarters in the historic town of Glen Jean, between Oak Hill and Beckley. HQ includes the old bank building that is one of the only remaining original structures of the town, registered on the National List of Historic Places. From here, head seven miles down to Thurmond on winding and narrow Route 25. On the way you can visit the popular Dunloup Creek Falls. The Cold Spot, just off the route in Glen Jean, is a convenient stop for wings, burgers, and cold drinks.

At the Glen Jean / Wood Mountain Rd traffic light on US 19, turn east, then immediately left (north) on Hwy 16/61. After 0.4 miles, turn right on Glen Jean Ln. Park HQ and the old bank will be obvious on both sides of the road. To go directly to Thurmond, take your first left (McKell Ave), before the bank, then immediately bear left again onto Thurmond Rd / Rt 25. Follow this on down — it's about 4.5 miles to Dunloup Creek Falls, 6.4 to Thurmond. There is a park visitor center in Thurmond, as well as various historic points of interest and a boat launch area. The (primitive) Stone Cliff campground is located about 1.7 miles upriver, before you cross the bridge. Reverse your route to return to Glen Jean, or, for the very adventurous in the right vehicle, there are the unpaved McKendree and Beury Mountain roads leading out of Thurmond that will allow you to make longer loops via Rt 41.

# Photography in the Park

## THE IMAGES BEHIND THE NRG GUIDE: ROBERT LEGG

Robert Legg is a West Virginia native. His search for meaning and beauty in life infiltrates the images he captures. Robert views photography as a way to record a memory of a moment and express a skill set, but says it's important to have fun with the process. The diverse landscape of the New River Gorge National Park and Preserve gives endless opportunities for photographs. For Robert, photographing the NRGNPP for this book was an opportunity to capture the park in its early stages as it continues to boom in popularity.

Robert says:
The best way to get started with landscape photography is to get out and do it. There's no correct way to do photography.

Anyone can be a photographer. The only difference between someone who is a photographer and someone who isn't — is just pulling out a camera and shooting.

The favorite photography spots located near major landmarks and viewpoints are popular for a reason. The New River Gorge Bridge, Grandview, and Hawks Nest Viewpoint all offer excellent scenes that truly define your location. While the major landmarks make for stunning imagery in themselves, the details can come to life with your own perspective and creativity.

The Bridge itself is an intricate engineering marvel and there are endless viewpoints and perspectives from which to capture its magnificence. And you can spend a lifetime taking shots of the New River watercourse itself, with its churning rapids and glistening rocks, and never get the same photo twice. Photography is a great way to immerse yourself in the natural environment, but do so mindfully. The park has lots of cliff ledges and unexpected slopes on the riverbanks. Be careful!

A few things to keep in mind to help your shooting:
- Your photos made into a gallery can be an amazing reminder of your visit. If you have a cell phone in your pocket, you're already a photographer waiting to tap into your potential.
- As you explore your surroundings, any time you feel an urge to take a photo of something, do it! Don't think too hard about how to get the perfect shot. Just take the picture!
- Each time of day and season provides different imagery; you can capture the park's changes through the days and seasons. The overall photography experience is boosted by the friendly NPS staff who can give you excellent location and trail recommendations.
- If you're serious, make a plan and a shot list. Include perspectives, times of day, landmarks, and more. Be aware of the weather, sunrise and sunset times, and sun exposures.
- If you plan to wait a while for specific shots in nature — birds, sunset or moon shots, etc. — bring supplies such as warmer clothes, snacks, and water.
- Pure landscape shots are pretty and good for practicing your craft, but adding people and action gives another layer of interest to your photos.
- You'll be surprised at how the imperfections in a photo can make it beautiful.

Scenic Drives

# SANDSTONE FALLS

The drive down to Hinton and back around to the Sandstone Falls Boardwalk is an ideal way to spend an afternoon — it's one of the only true riverside drives in the park. Access via I-64, either from Beckley to the west, or on your way into the region from the east, starting at the Sandstone Visitor Center right off the highway. The route follows WV 20 as it runs along the east side of the river, climbs up past some spectacular overlooks, then drops back down to the town of Hinton, where a bridge takes you across to a riverside drive on the other side of the New that brings you north to Sandstone Falls Boardwalk. You have several options for the return.

- The roads: good two-lane on Rt 20 and New River Rd; narrow and unpaved for six miles on Irish Mountain (optional).
- Distance: 20 miles and 40 minutes one-way; 30 miles and a little over an hour for the Irish Mountain loop.

From I-64, take exit 139 and turn left (south) on Rt 20. Alternately, turn right and first check out the Sandstone Visitor Center — it's just a few hundred feet from the exit. Here you can learn about the New River region through interactive exhibits, see native flowers in the Monarch Butterfly Garden, view a short film about the New River, or browse books and gifts.

After passing the Sandstone General Store, you'll climb up out of the river bottom. Approximately three miles from I-64 you'll be 600 feet above the New River at the Sandstone Falls scenic overlook. From the parking lot a short gravel walkway leads to this remarkable viewpoint.

After the overlook you'll descend back to river level; at this point you'll pass the turnoff to the Three Rivers Avian Center up Brooks Mountain Road (see page 39). A few miles later you'll reach Hinton — 10.5 miles from the interstate exit and about 20 minutes without stops.

Sandstone Falls.

In Hinton you'll find a variety of eateries and the Hinton Railroad Museum, skateboarding lessons at Sk8it, movies at the restored Ritz Theater, gifts at Otter & Oak, and a great little park at Brookside Roadside Park. It's a fun litle town and a good place to stay a night or two.

From Hinton you'll cross over the New River and, turn right onto WV 26/New River Rd. From Hinton, it's nine more miles and about 20 minutes to get to the Sandstone Falls Boardwalk. Along the way you'll pass the trailheads for the Big Branch and the Fall Branch Trails, both very pretty trails with waterfalls.

At the Boardwalk you'll find a stroller- and wheelchair-accessible trail that crosses two bridges leading to fishing areas, islands, and observation decks with outstanding views of the river and falls.

After enjoying yourself at Sandstone Falls you can retrace your route back to Hinton and Beckley or you can brave the unpaved Irish Mountain Road directly back to I-64. For that option, from the Boardwalk parking area, continue northeast on New River Rd for 0.3 miles, then turn left onto Irish Mountain Rd. Follow this adventurous little backroad for 6.3 miles to a T-interscetion at Pluto Rd. Turn right and drive about a mile to I-64. You'll come out at exit 133, six miles closer to Beckley than where you exited the highway at Sandstone.

Irish Mountain Road is a classic, winding WV dirt road. It has a few rough spots, navigable in the average vehicle, but not recommended for RVs, trailers, or any lowered or oversize vehicle. Named for the Irish immigrants who settled here and farmed, Irish Mountain's summit is 2691 feet, about 1000 feet above the river. The little church and cemetary two miles in was built in 1878 and was the first Roman Catholic church in Raleigh County. (The church is open; you can go in to take pictures and/or say a prayer.)

# HIKING & BIKING

Somewhere New.

**Exploring the trails** is one of the best ways to get a real feel for the park. Trails in the NRGPP range from flat quarter-mile strolls to brutally steep stairways descending into the heart of the gorge — something for just about every type of visitor. The Park Service gives fairly detailed information about many hikes on its website, and dedicated hiking books are available. Exceptionally ambitious and/or regular visitors may be interested in joining the 100-Mile Challenge, which rewards hikers who complete 100 miles of hiking — over any period of time. If you're uncertain about hiking or want to stroll along with running commentary from a local, you can even charter a guided hike through ACE Adventure Resort.

## BACKPACKING IN THE PARK

The NRGPP region isn't known for extensive tracts of remote wilderness, but it's still possible to get far enough out to warrant a night under the stars. The best trails for backpacking are probably those in the Glade Creek area between Beckley and Sandstone. Group size in undeveloped backcountry areas is limited to two tents and eight people, and other restrictions also apply. Check at the visitor centers or the NPS website for up-to-date information.

### Going Further

If you're serious about hiking in the park, *Hiking & Biking in the New River Gorge National Park and Preserve* by Bryan Simon is the book for you, with over 100 trails and 350 pages of detailed trail information by an expert local. This covers not just the park proper, but the entire region from Summersville in the north to Pipestem in the south. Available at local shops or from Wolverine Publishing.

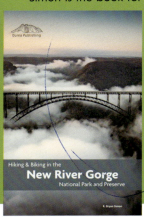

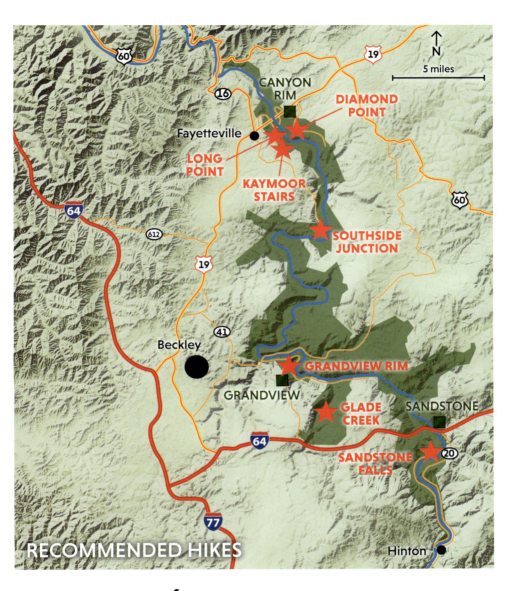

# Beat the Heat

It's mid-summer. Hot. Humid. But you have places to go and sights to see. Caution! If you find yourself sweating profusely, take time to cool down in the shade. Stay hydrated — preferably by sipping water or electrolyte drinks every 10 minutes. Everyone is at risk for dehydration, heat exhaustion, and heat stroke, but especially children, the elderly, those with underlying health conditions, and people who are really exerting themselves on hot and humid days.

Dress in layers so you can easily shed them. Wear a hat to keep the sun off your head and use cooling neck towels or head bands. On hot days, choose hikes in the shade and pace yourself — start out slowly to gauge the heat's effect. Mid-hike, remember that being in nature is why you are here. Stop to take breaks, drink water, eat snacks, enjoy the view, and take pictures.

## RECOMMENDED HIKES

Covering all the park's trails is way beyond the scope of this book, but here are some enduring favorites, starting with the easiest. See the locator map on the previous page.

### Sandstone Falls

The broad cascades of Sandstone Falls form the largest waterfall on the New River, a sight that should not be missed. Reach a mid-channel island via this half-mile boardwalk stroll that is wheelchair- and stroller-friendly. At its end, enjoy observation decks with fine views of the falls as well as access to fishing areas.

This trail begins at the endpoint of the Sandstone Falls scenic drive — see page 70.

### Grandview Rim Trail

This 1.6-mile one-way hike starts at the Grandview Main Overlook parking area and hikes the rim of the gorge to the Turkey Spur Overlook. Follow the signs and the paved path out toward the scenic Main Overlook, then head left. This trail is perfect if you have members of

## Tough Footing

The park features some pretty rough terrain, which is part of what makes it such an fun place to explore. Your feet are mainly responsible for transporting you around the New, so outfit them properly. In the summer months, light hiking shoes or hiking sandals are much preferred over flip-flops or street shoes. Trekking poles can help you keep your balance, and save your knees when going up or down steep slopes. Tripping hazards such as rocks and exposed roots are common, and gorge-rim trails often lead to the edges of cliffs. Guard rails are rare in the park! Always keep a safe distance from the cliff edge when you are enjoying the view — especially when taking selfies!

Grandview.

your party who don't want to hike and would rather shuttle the car but still enjoy the views. Alternatively, make it a 3.2-mile roundtrip. Located 1400 feet above the river, Grandview features many other short, moderate hikes, as well as a route to hike or bike down to the river. If you're an early riser, arrive at the trailhead before dawn for one of the most spectacular sunrises you've ever seen.

From I-64 eastbound, take exit 129B for County Rt 9 N/Grandview Rd. Follow Grandview Rd for 5.3 miles to the visitor center.

## Southside Junction Trail

Named for a junction of railroad tracks at its southern end, this out-and-back jaunt starts in Cunard and follows the old railroad line south through the gorge. You'll be near the river the whole time. Easy to navigate and with a total elevation gain of less than 30 feet, it's perfect for the less ambitious — or you can make it into a long, flat trail run or bike ride. From Cunard, follow a gravel road upstream as it narrows into a tree-covered trail. Along the way you'll see remnants of old coal works and towns, as well as wildlife and flowers. You can go seven miles one-way all the way to the bridge at Thurmond, but just go as long as you like before turning around. Note that the drive down to the river is narrow and winding.

From US 16 just south of Fayetteville fork left onto Gatewood Rd. Go 4.5 miles (to Gatewood) and turn left onto Cunard Road. Drive 1.8 miles (to Cunard) and turn left onto County Rt 9/14; go 100 yards and turn left onto Cunard River Access Rd; follow this for 1.6 miles down to the river and trailhead.

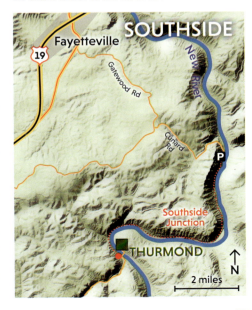

## Selfie Safety

My photos of people taking selfies in the gorge were some of the most fun photos that I took. Taking selfies, whether you are alone or with a group, is a great way to capture beautiful memories, but it can't be said enough — use caution when taking them! Cliffs, rocks, water, and exposed roots all present dangers, especially when you are focused on angles and looking through the lens. At the cliff top you risk not only slipping and falling, but you can also knock off debris that could harm climbers on the cliffs and hikers below. When you are by water, be aware of and respect the swift current. Riverside rocks are notoriously slippery, even if they appear dry; if your shoe is wet, you can easily slip unexpectedly. Stay aware of where you are, your surroundings, and of others. No photo is worth hurting yourself or others.

— Robert Legg

### Diamond Point

A short drive out Lansing-Edmond Road from the Canyon Rim Visitor Center takes you to a marked trailhead for Endless Wall/Diamond Point. A 2.4-mile out-and-back, this hike is moderate in difficulty and arrives at a stunning vista of the gorge. The trail starts in an unusual grove of old-growth pines, later crossing picturesque Fern Creek and climbing gently to the rim of the gorge. There is a second Endless Wall trailhead about a half mile farther east along Lansing-Edmond Road; if you don't mind a bit of road walking you can follow the rim of the gorge, return to the road at the other trailhead, and make a loop of it.

From the Canyon Rim Visitor Center, take US 19 0.3 miles north, then turn right on Lansing-Edmond Rd. Go 1.7 miles — the parking lot and trailhead is on the right, at the bottom of the dip.

### Long Point

This all-time classic gives a panoramic view of the gorge and the bridge. It starts at its own trailhead off Gatewood Rd, or you can start in Fayetteville via the Fayetteville Trail for a much longer outing. You can also start at the Kaymoor trailhead — there are lots of options in this area! The standard hike is 3.2 miles roundtrip and quite moderate, but be careful on the actual point, a rock outcropping with cliffs on three sides and no guardrails.

To reach the trailhead, go south on US 16 through Fayetteville; about a quarter mile past

Long Point vista.

Cathedral Cafe, fork left onto Gatewood Rd. Drive 1.8 miles, then take a left onto Newton Rd; go 200 yards to the trailhead parking.

## The Kaymoor Stairs

Mile for mile, this may be the most strenuous trail in the NRG — or anywhere! Starting at the Kaymoor trailhead out Gatewood Rd, it drops more than 800 vertical feet from rim to river, with an average grade of 30%, (42.5% on the long stairs section!). From the rim you'll wander down through switchbacks, passing some steep cliffs (watch for rock climbers!), waterfalls, and mine ruins before descending the elaborate staircase of 821 steps. While now very overgrown, the Kaymoor Mine site at the bottom still has interesting mining machinery and infrastructure. The spectacular views of the gorge and the cliffs of Endless Wall across the way will distract you from the lung-and-quad burn you are about to experience going back up!

To reach the trailhead, go south on US 16 through Fayetteville; about a quarter mile past Cathedral Cafe, fork left onto Gatewood Rd. Drive for 1.9 miles and take a left onto Kaymoor Rd (just past the turn for Long Point parking). Go 1 mile to the T-intersection and take a left to parking and the trailhead sign.

## BIKING

Road biking around the NRGPP is challenging and beautiful, but not for everyone. Narrow roads, blind curves, alternating sun and shade, and the rarity of bike traffic put riders at great risk from vehicle traffic. Consider yourself warned! That said, the New is increasingly popular for mountain biking. There's a wide variety of terrain in the park, from beginner to advanced. Additionally, there are many local bike shops and outfitters offering rentals and guided biking tours. Here are a few of the park's mountain-biking highlights.

### Arrowhead Trails

Built by kids for kids, the Arrowhead Trails were constructed by over 1000 Boy Scouts, the largest youth service project in park history. This Kaymoor-area playground features over 12 miles of well-marked single-track trails with various natural obstacles. For beginners, the one-mile **Clovis Trail** lets young cyclists build basic skills. The 2.9-mile **Adena Trail** offers more challenges, while the **Dalton** and **LeCroy** trails up the ante even more.

From the town of Fayetteville, head south on US 16 and turn left onto Gatewood Rd, travel 1.9 miles and turn left onto Kaymoor Rd, drive a mile and take a right at the T-intersection, and the parking lot is at the end of the road.

### Glade Creek Trail

An out-and-back hiking and biking trail, at just over 11 miles roundtrip (5.6 miles one way), this is a moderately difficult biking trail that follows the old narrow-gauge railroad line up Glade Creek. The trail winds through a hardwood forest and has plenty of rhododendrons as well as swimming holes.

From US 19 south of Oak Hill, take the Glen

Jean exit. Turn right (south) onto Route 61 and go 2.8 miles. Turn left, staying on Route 61, and continue for another 4.6 miles. Turn left onto Route 41 and go four miles toward Prince, then turn right (just before the bridge) onto Glade Creek Rd. Follow the gravel road seven miles to the Glade Creek trailhead.

## Babcock State Park

Located just 20 minutes from the Canyon Rim Visitor Center, Babcock is a go-to spot in the region for more advanced riders. There are currently 11 trails open to mountain bikers, with many loops possible.

To reach the park from the visitor center, go north on US 19 for 4.9 miles and exit at US 60/Midland Trail. At the end of the exit ramp, go left and travel 5.5 miles south to County Rt 11. Turn right and go 3.8 miles to the park entrance.

## Other Options

At Grandview, you can ride the Little Laurel Trail that drops 1400 feet to the river, possibly connecting up with the Glade Creek ride described above — a shuttle is nice for this one! The casual **Southside Junction** hike described on page 75 is also open to biking. Biking is also permitted on the **Bluestone Turnpike Trail** at Bluestone National Scenic River, and there are mountain biking trails at Summersville Lake and Little Beaver State Park.

## Stay Found

Exploring a new area is fun and exciting, but figuring out the lay of the land takes some effort. Spend some time with a good old-fashioned map, as cell service is notoriously hit or miss in the hills. Use your phone to carry screen shots of directions and maps if you don't want to bring paper. No matter if you're traveling alone or with a group, always inform someone outside your party where you're going and when you expect to be back, a simple precaution that can bring help even if you can't call for it yourself.

# HUNTING & FISHING

## HUNTING
The park allows hunting of turkey, black bear, and whitetail deer, among other animals. Special restrictions will apply. If you plan on doing any hunting in the park, research both the National Park Service's guidelines and those of the state of West Virginia, as license violations can result in hefty fines. The National Park Service website has in-depth information on hunting guidelines and restrictions. Be sure to check for the most up-to-date information regarding areas that are closed to hunting. The West Virginia Department of Natural Resources website — wvdnr.gov — has thorough information about hunting within the state.

## FISHING
Nothing beats a day casting along the riverbank, and the New River Gorge area can offer plenty such days. Note that some areas of the river are catch-and-release zones.

Common fish types of the area include crappie, walleye, bluegill, trout, and four kinds of bass. Remember, catching the coveted largemouth bass is less about special lures and more about what type of angler you are.

For West Virginia fishing license information, visit the website of the state's Department of Natural Resources: wvdnr.gov/buy-a-license/. WVDNR offers annual, lifetime, and seniors fishing licenses. If you're only in the area for a few days, the tourist license is good for three days. See also Hunting and Fishing Outfitters on page 112.

## Survival & Bushcraft

Looking to learn survival skills? New River Survival and Bushcraft can teach you how to be prepared for the unexpected in the outdoors. Offering full- and half-day courses on survival, bushcraft, bugout, and BSA Wilderness Survival Merit Badge, NRS&B offers something for the whole family. Courses teach navigation, survival mindset, firecraft, campcraft, and more. www.newriversurvival.com

# Leave No Trace

A main principle of the Leave No Trace philosophy is, whatever you pack in, you pack out. Remember to bring a spare bag to pack out your trash, including food scraps. Scan your picnic area or campsite for microtrash — little bits of waste that can easily be missed, such as cigarette butts, gum wrappers, and the tiny plastic strips that seal bottle caps.

While you might assume it's OK to throw food scraps or organic waste on the ground, it really isn't. Orange peels, for example, decompose extremely slowly and can remain unsightly all season. Even more important than aesthetics is the effect of discarded food on the park's animals. Human food sources disrupt an animal's food preferences, and can make it sick or damage its ability to seek out natural food. Additionally, feeding animals or leaving food out can cause wildlife to associate humans with food, which can lead to dangerous encounters with animals ranging from raccoons to black bears. Bears that have become habituated to humans are often euthanized. Keep a clean camp, save a bear.

# PADDLING & CLIMBING

## PADDLING THE NEW

The New River is famous for its whitewater, but you don't need to be an experienced rafter or kayaker to enjoy it. Commercial outfitters are one of the area's most important industries. They provide experienced guides, boats, shuttles, and all the safety equipment you need for a trip down the river — and depending how long the trip, they also do meals and drinks. Commercial trips on the New range from a few hours to two days. Although flatwater paddlers can put in as far upstream as Hinton, the more exciting part begins at McCreery, where Rt 41 crosses the river below Grandview overlook. Below here, the river is traditionally

Raft-guide-turned-writer Jay Young dives deep into river running in his history, *Whitewater Rafting West Virginia's New and Gauley Rivers*. From the days of batteaux to the modern days of rafting, expect to be introduced to the wild stories and characters who braved the rapids and turned wild whitewater into a fun recreational activity. Available in local shops.

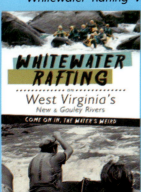

divided into two sections, the "Upper" and the "Lower" New.

The Upper New, from McCreery to Thurmond, is a family-friendly 12-mile trip you might consider doing on your own if you have the gear and a bit of whitewater experience. This section features Class I and Class II rapids (some say up to Class III at high water levels). Commercial trips are open to kids ages six and above, and many allow you to paddle your own inflatable kayak. The Upper New features long pools, with numerous fun and easy rapids, and is great for camping and fishing, too. Trip lengths vary depending on the season and water levels.

The Lower New, a 14-mile run from Thurmond (or 7 miles from Cunard) to Fayette Station, features big, powerful rapids. Private trips are for very experienced whitewater boaters only. Rapids range from Class III to Class V, and at some water levels the current creates thundering holes that are truly awe inspiring. Commercial trips are open to paddlers ages 12 and older who want to experience big fun and wild whitewater.

Outfitters offer two-hour "express" trips, full-day trips on each section, and two-day trips that run both the Upper and Lower with a night camping on the riverbank. Many outfitters have packages where you can combine a whitewater trip with other activities such as horseback riding or rappelling.

When you go rafting, depending on the season, dress smart. Wear swimsuits under shorts, and synthetic shirts for summer. In cooler months, wetsuits are highly recommended (outfitters can often provide them), and a light windbreaker or synthetic pullover

is often welcome anytime. A good water shoe or sandal will stay on your feet; flip-flops won't. Sunglasses are recommended, but wear a sunglass strap — sunglasses don't float! Don't forget your sunscreen. If you insist on taking your phone, make sure it has a good waterproof case and/or have your guide keep it in a drybag.

## The Gauley

Located just north of the park proper and joining the New at Gauley Bridge, the Gauley is one of the wildest commercially run whitewater rivers in the country. Just the names of some of the Class V rapids here bring a thrill to river runners nationwide: Iron Ring, Sweets Falls, Pillow Rock. Check YouTube for a look at the action. Beginning in September, the water in Summersville Lake (a large man-made reservoir on the Gauley) is released into the river, providing exciting, high-volume flows: Gauley Season! If you're a strong paddler and swimmer, and the Lower New felt too tame, consider a trip down the Gauley. Like the New, the Gauley is traditionally split into two sections, Upper and Lower. Both are Class V, with the Upper being significantly wilder.

## Kayaking

If you've ever wanted to try kayaking, there are plenty of options to learn either flatwater or whitewater kayaking skills from an experienced instructor. With lessons available on the Upper New, or Summersville and Hawks Nest lakes, you'll learn paddle strokes, how to "read" whitewater, and how to roll a kayak. Outfitters keep class sizes small, so you'll get plenty of instruction and feedback.

## SUP

If you haven't tried stand-up paddleboarding (SUP), this might be your chance! SUP has been gaining popularity in recent years, and

Fisherfolk and whitewater rafters may want to check the U.S. Geological Survey website for up-to-date information on the area's current water levels.
waterdata.usgs.gov/wv/nwis/current/?type=flow

Paddling & Climbing    83

# Rock n' Road

Mike Williams, rock climber, spent over a decade living in a self-built camper van and visiting climbing areas from New Hampshire to Yosemite. He finally declared the New River Gorge to be the best climbing of all, and made Fayetteville home. Years later, Mike authored *New River Rock*, a rock-climbing guide to the New, Meadow, and Gauley river gorges, now in its third edition and expanded to two volumes. His excellent books are available at local shops, or from Wolverine Publishing. Mike — along with his wife Elissa (also an expert rock climber) and two children Hazel and Elliott now own a house near the rim of the gorge. Most recently Mike founded **Bridge Bound Campers**, a custom van-conversion shop located in downtown Fayetteville.

offers the perfect combination of exercise and on-the-water sunshine. It's a fun way to test your balance and core strength, too. Guided trips are offered on the Upper New and at Summersville Lake. Some tours require a minimum age or minimum number of participants when booking. Summersville Lake is a large and beautiful lake north of the New, with clear water and surrounded by striking cliffs — the perfect place to try paddleboarding for the first time before advancing to moving water.

## ROCK CLIMBING

Are you ready to see things from (literally) a new angle? With over 3000 roped and bouldering routes, the New is a legendary climbing destination. If you're an experienced climber ... you already know about the steep and perfect Nuttall Sandstone. If not, consider hiring a climbing guide to show you the ropes. There are several reputable guide services in the area that cater to both beginners and experienced climbers, so you can sign up for a day at your skill level. Age restrictions vary, so inquire when booking a family adventure. There is an American Alpine Club campground especially for climbers located near the Junkyard crag off Ames Heights Rd.

# ADVENTURES WITH KIDS

**When you love the outdoors**, it's natural to want to share your appreciation for nature with young children. Kids, of course, see it differently. The trick is to ensure you're passing along appreciation instead of resentment. What's the difference between an easy, happy, fun-filled adventure and one filled with resistant and whining kids? The answer is ... no one knows. Nevertheless, pack more water, drinks, and snacks than your kids could possibly eat. Also, unexpected things happen! Bring a small first aid kit, flashlight, and extra clothes.

All that said, having fun adventures with your kids is easy in the park. Here are our top adventures for you and your kiddos to enjoy:

## Burnwood Trail
The perfect hiking trail for little legs, the 1.2-mile Burnwood loop is an easy hike through the old-growth forest. The trail starts in a small field — perfect for a basecamp and picnic — before leading you into the lush forest. Start at the Burnwood Group Campsite area directly across US 19 from the Canyon Rim Visitor Center (picnic shelters, toilets, water). The trailhead is just northwest of the parking area.

## John Henry Monument Museum and Gift Shop
The legend of the "Steel Drivin' Man" John Henry has captured imaginations for generations. Said to be seven feet tall and able to do the work of seven men, John Henry is a true folk hero. Kids can walk along the Greenbrier River to view the Big Bend Tunnel and learn about John Henry, the man and the legend. Located along Route 3 east of Hinton.

## Arrowhead Bike Farm Pump Track
The practice pump-track is great for kids learning to mountain bike, plus they have goats the kids can look at and feed, and craft beer for adults. Bike rentals are available at the full-service shop. Located near Kaymoor — for more info on Arrowhead, see page 78.

## Fayetteville Town Park Loop
The one-mile town park loop is super fun. It has a little stream that is fun to play in or

In the Bridge.

observe, and if you have a mixed group, more adventurous hikers can head out on connecting trails to Kaymoor or Long Point.

## Tree Tops Tour
An aerial park at Adventures on the Gorge, open to kids ages 10 and up, featuring ziplines, swinging sky bridges, and elevated ladders. Kids are helmeted and harnessed before ascending into the leafy forest canopy, and will gain confidence as they navigate transitions and fly through the air.

## ACE Waterpark
Cool down at this spring-fed waterpark at the ACE Adventure Resort basecamp in Minden. Surrounded by lush green trees, with a white sand beach and giant inflatable toys, it's perfect for even the littlest adventurers. With floating waterpads, trampolines, twin waterslides, a zipline, and the notorious launch pad known as the BLOB, this is the perfect place to stay cool. Wood-fired pizza, drinks, and snacks are only a minute away, so it's fun for parents, too.

## Bridge Walk
For kids ages eight and up. A thrilling, airy, three-hour tour that gives an amazing view of the structural and engineering marvel that is the New River Gorge Bridge. Kids (and you) will really get an appreciation for the magnitude of the gorge.

### Mountain State Miniature Golf
Located in Beckley. Little ones can enjoy 18 holes of miniature golf, while learning the history of different points in West Virginia. It's fun and educational.

### Junior Ranger
The NPS Junior Ranger program lets kids interactively learn about the park while also helping NPS rangers protect it. Stop by any visitor center and ask a ranger for a workbook to get started. Once kids complete the Junior Ranger book and activities, they get a certificate and a badge.

### Teen Rock-Climbing Camp
Does your kid belong to a climbing gym back home? For kids ages 12-17 who are motivated climbers, the Teen Climbing Camp offered by New River Mountain Guides teaches your kid the techniques and skills to safely climb outdoors. Plus, they'll get to pitch their own tent, camp under the stars, and enjoy s'mores around the campfire.
www.newriverclimbing.com/kids-programs

### Escapatorium
Need a rain-day activity? Located in downtown Fayetteville, the indoor adventures at Escapatorium challenge you and your family to beat the clock, find the clues, and make your "escape." With multiple scenarios to choose from, this is truly a "New" reality for everyone to enjoy. escape-a-torium.com

## Charlie Chipmunk

Fayetteville local, Melanie Seiler is the founding Executive Director of Active Southern West Virginia (www.activeswv.org) and has over 20 years recreating in the outdoors. A certified instructor in stand-up paddle boarding, telemark skiing, and river guiding, she is the author of *Charlie Chipmunk Plays Outside*, a kids book that details Leave No Trace Principles.
www.amazon.com/author/wvmelanie

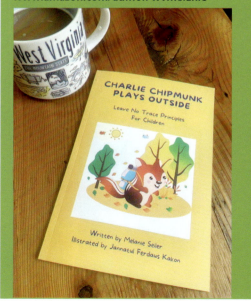

# AMENITIES

# LODGING

**Your choice of lodging** can have a big impact on your experience in the park, so plan ahead. No matter where you stay, be sure to book well ahead of time if visiting in peak season. Events such as Bridge Day and Gauley Season can make last-minute arrangements especially difficult. The time of year can also affect prices, so if you're staying in a hotel or resort, an off-season visit can save you quite a bit.

The New River Gorge region has countless lodging options, from primitive campgrounds to rustic cabins, Airbnbs, rafting resorts, standard hotels, even luxury resorts. There are various factors to consider when choosing.

First, the time of year and weather. If visiting in the fall, are you comfortable camping in the cold? If a chilly mountain evening can ruin your day, you might want to splurge a little for something indoors. Similarly, if hot and humid afternoons are torture, consider an air-conditioned room. Location is another important factor. Do you love early morning and late evening hikes? Some lodging options allow you to hike directly from your campsite or room without getting in the car. If you're enthusiastic about the local food scene, consider staying right in Fayetteville, where you can walk to many restaurants. If you absolutely need a Hilton or Marriott, Beckley is your best bet.

## CAMPING IN THE PARK

The NRGNPP does not have the usual national-park-style, full-amenity campgrounds. Instead, the official park campgrounds offer no-fee, primitive camping, first come, first served. Sites cannot be reserved and are located well off the beaten path, all but one along the New River. They are primitive camping areas that do not offer drinking water or hookups, and have limited restroom facilities. Many cushier developed campgrounds are available nearby, including those at various river outfitters and state parks.

**Official park campgrounds are, from north to south:**

- Brooklyn — Near the Cunard River Access.
- Stone Cliff — A mile and a half upstream from Thurmond, near the McKendree Rd bridge.
- Thayer — Across the river and a few miles upstream from Stone Cliff, along the rugged McKendree Road.
- Army Camp — Across the river and downstream from the McCreery river access on Rt 41.
- Grandview Sandbar — A bit upstream from McCreery, directly below Grandview.
- War Ridge — Not along the river; past McCreery along Rt 41, then out Backus Mountain Rd.
- Glade Creek — Farther upstream from McCreery past Grandview Sandbar, near the Glade Creek Trailhead.
- Meadow Creek — Probably the easiest NPS campground to get to, just north of the Sandstone Visitor Center.

## OTHER LODGING

The river outfitters have a long tradition of providing camping and lodging, and give you a lot of options. Adventures on the Gorge (AOTG), Cantrell Ultimate Rafting, New and Gauley River Adventures, West Virginia Adventures, and ACE all offer camping and cabin rentals in addition to their whitewater trips.

At **AOTG** you can camp, let the kids play at the playground, take a yoga class overlooking the gorge, and enjoy drinks and dinner at Smokey's. **ACE** has over 50 cabins, and from any of them you can hit a bike trail, go ziplining, or enjoy the waterpark — all without getting in your car. **Cantrell's** has tent and RV camping, cabins, and a restaurant. Located close to Thurmond, **West Virginia Adventures** has campsites, RV camping, and cabins. **New and Gauley River Adventures** has camping at their basecamp off Lansing Road and also has a sweet cottage on the New River at Thurmond, with a large deck overlooking the water and a hot tub.

There are countless cabin-rental options in the New River Gorge area. Here are a few of our favorites — look them up and see which one might be right for you.

- Opossum Creek Retreat
- Hemlock Haven
- Dogwood Cabins
- Country Road Cabins
- New River Cabins
- Country River Inn
- Morris Harvey House
- Millcreek Cabins

# STATE PARKS NEAR NRGNPP

**A lot of the nearby** state parks offer great accommodations as well, plus a multitude of outdoor pursuits in spectacular settings. Here are some to check out:

## BABCOCK STATE PARK
Located just 20 minutes from the Canyon Rim Visitor Center, this is the most centrally located of the nearby state parks. You'll find 4000 acres of wilderness to enjoy, as well as 52 campsites (including RV parking), laundry facilities, and showers. You can also rent cabins with wood-burning fireplaces as well as cooking supplies (pets NOT permitted, unfortunately). These make an ideal, low-stress weekend getaway for couples and families alike. Even if you don't stay in Babcock, don't miss the Glade Creek Grist Mill, one of the region's most visited attractions. (Spoiler: the mill is a replica, built in the mid-1970s after the older Cooper's Mill that was destroyed by fire. It is, however, in working order and very photogenic, so be sure to stop by and snap some pictures.)

## HAWKS NEST STATE PARK
This smaller park located 20 minutes north of Fayetteville makes an ideal day trip. With over 270 acres within its limits, there are numerous activities for visitors to enjoy during their stay. You can take a jetboat tour, ride an aerial tram, hike, or bike. There's camping and a restaurant.

## LITTLE BEAVER STATE PARK
If you prefer a bit more solitude, consider driving out to Little Beaver State Park. This little wilderness spot is near the southwest region of New River Gorge National Park and Preserve, about six miles east of Beckley. There are 16 seasonal campsites (on weekends you

Babcock State Park.

may be required to book two nights, so keep that in mind before reserving) plus a camp store with firewood, ice, and Wi-Fi. This 500-acre park feature many hiking trails.

## BLUESTONE STATE PARK
Located south of Hinton and the Sandstone Visitor Center near Bluestone Lake and Bluestone National Scenic River, this state park has 120 campsites sprinkled about, some appropriate for RVs while some are primitive and must be reached by boat. There are also cabins at Bluestone State Park accommodating up to eight people, some allowing pets (specify when booking).

## PIPESTEM RESORT STATE PARK
This is a big (4000-acre) park featuring all kinds of attractions, including a tramway that reaches 3600 feet, ziplining, horseback riding tours, the 18-hole golf course, a lake with splash park, kayaking, paddleboarding, and guided bike trips. Winter is also a popular time to visit, as the park has great terrain for cross-country skiing and sledding (you can rent equipment on-site).

# EATING

**It's no secret** that the New River Gorge region has a thriving food scene. West Virginia has a centuries-old tradition of turning simple ingredients into delicious meals. A typical day in the Appalachian Mountains involved hard physical work, and a savory meal followed by a sweet dessert was essential. The result was a rich tradition of homemade food and food preservation that bonded communities with the seasons and the land, drawing from a number of Old World and African immigrant cultures. Favorites in the hills include pinto beans and corn bread, biscuits and gravy, venison, smoked trout, berry cobbler, pepperoni rolls, and hot dogs with chili and slaw.

With the meals often came finely crafted drinks, followed by music and dancing. Today visitors can recreate the experience of dining within the community by visiting the many eateries that continue the old traditions of eating regional foods and drinking artisanal beverages. Bring your best appetite to these locally owned and operated businesses, all of which have outstanding service and food. Ask about and try the specials, which often feature local in-season ingredients. For those with a sweet tooth, don't miss the carrot cake at Cathedral Cafe, peanut-butter terrine at Pies & Pints, and ice cream at The Stache — all in Fayetteville — and the lemon bars at Custom Creations Bakery in Oak Hill.

Many places are closed in the winter or have reduced hours, so when in doubt call ahead. And if you have a cabin with cooking facilities, in season there are many farmer's markets that can add local freshness to your meals.

## Local Chef

Joy Marr was fresh out of college, following her dream to work outdoors when she moved to West Virginia to work as a raft guide. She remembers, "I passed the river-guide training and was paid extra to cook meals four days a week for the staff, as well as organize the lunch foods, which consisted of iceberg lettuce, tomatoes, bologna and salami, peanut butter, apples, and breads. This bumped my lowly first-year guide pay into the second-year slot as I perfected my meals for 10-15 guides in the mini kitchen of a 12-foot tin-can travel trailer." As a guide Joy learned about confluence — the joining of two rivers. She quickly realized the confluence of food, adventure, and life in the New River Gorge. Joy still guided but became the local go-to gal for random cooking questions, supporter of farmers, farmers markets, and early adopter of health and wellness as a reflection of ourselves. Today Joy can be found working on her upcoming cookbook or teaching Pilates at **Activated Body Studio** in Oak Hill.

## LOCAL EATERIES

### Fayetteville Area

Fayetteville is a well-known foodie town and offers something for everyone, from vegan takeout to international cuisine to regional ramp dishes — plus a wide variety of settings. We can't list every good restaurant, but here is a generous portion of favorites.

**Pies and Pints** — A Fayetteville institution. Handcrafted pizza, delicious salads, wings, and extravagant desserts in a modern dining room. Great beer list, including many locally brewed and draft. (304) 574-2200

**Secret Sandwich Society** – At press time, SSS was still rebuilding after a fire — hopefully by the time you read this you'll know why this was/is one of the 'ville's favorite eateries. Soups,

Pies at Pies.

sandwiches, burgers, house-made pickles and chips. Their loaded fries, topped with pimento cheese, bacon, and jalapenos, are worth a drive to the New. (304) 640-8152

**Cathedral Café / Raw & Juicy Juice Bar** — One of Fayetteville's oldest and dearest, the Cathedral has been serving breakfast, lunch, and dinner for decades. The old church location is funky and charming, and the menu features classic favorites: pancakes, bagel sandwiches, cinnamon buns, salads, and sandwiches. A great meet-up spot, and at a back table someone is always working on the crossword. (304) 574-0202

**Wood Iron Eatery** — Enjoy the Bad Kid Coffee that is roasted on-site, alongside waffles, tofu scrambles, house-made sausage, and candied bacon. (304) 900-5557

**Southside Junction & Tap House** — Food and more fun than most restaurants you've been too. Darts, pool, beer, great pub food, live music, and the occasional drag show. (304) 574-2222

**Wanderlust Creativefoods** — Fusion at its finest. High-quality hand-picked dishes from around the world, served at an affordable cost and a fast pace. Mussels, ribeye, curries, and more. (304) 574-3111

**Firecreek BBQ & Steaks** — Featuring outdoor dining — if it can be grilled or BBQed, this is the place! Don't miss Ribeye Tuesdays. (304) 900-5505

**The Handle Bar @ Arrowhead Bike Farm** — Beer, bikes, food, and buskers. A casual eatery with daily specials and a pump track for the kiddos. (304) 900-5501

**Our House Grill & Pub @ Cantrell's** — A lively eatery offering homemade sauces and fresh-made house specials. Hosts live entertainment throughout the rafting season. (304) 877-8235

**The Burrito Bar at Breeze Hill** — Featuring a river-rapid-inspired menu. Savory tacos, burritos, quesadillas, beer and wine, and stunning sunset views. (304) 574-2750

**Adventures on the Gorge** — Several styles of dining at this sprawling rafting resort. Try Smokey's for an overlook of the gorge, a sizzling steak, and a glass of Cabernet. Hit Chetty's for a great selection of drafts and pub food like fried pepperoni rolls and chicken wings. Java Falls Cafe is a good place to start the day with coffee and grab-and-go lunch options. The Snack Shack has ice cream and pool-side snacks. (304) 461-6570

# Local Brews & Wines

**FREEFOLK BREWERY**
The folks at Freefolk Brewery, Jeff and Sarah Edwards, are both native West Virginians. Jeff began brewing beer in his Morgantown backyard in 2014, on a 15-gallon system that he pieced together from yard sales. What started as a hobby soon turned into a passion, and soon he was making some pretty good homebrew. Then he took the craft to the next level — that's how Freefolk got started. The Freefolk team filled the brewery with handcrafted steel features, wood, blacksmithing, concrete, and covered every inch of the walls with painted murals that pay homage to the West Virginian culture of music and spirit. The taproom is a key element at Freefolk; they brew and serve beer in an environment designed to be comfortable, inspiring, and fun. They host live music and pop-up kitchens, too. www.freefolkbrew.com

**BRIDGE BREW WORKS**
Offering a variety of seasonal and year-round brews. Favorites include Three River Triple, Mountain Momma Pale Ale, Longpoint Lager and Shay's Revenge. Located near Fayetteville, you can tour the brewery and try a flight of local brews in the tasting room.

**DOBRA ZUPAS**
Located near Beckley, this brewery is located in an old house and features a full-service restaurant. Local favorites include: WyCo Wheat, Barkers Ridge Blonde, and Hopped-up IPA. The menu changes seasonally but you can always count on wings, salads, pizzas, burgers, and steaks.

**DANIEL VINEYARDS**
Located southwest of Beckley (near the Twin Oaks Golf Course), this conservation grape farm is a family-owned estate winery. Featuring award-winning wines made from Norton, Marquette, Frontenac, Petite, and Pearl Red grapes, they also have berry dessert wines and port — and a tasting room.

**ACE Whitewater** — The Lost Paddle Bar and Grill offers indoor and patio dining overlooking ACE lake. Wood-fired pizza, black Angus burgers, wings, classic cocktails, and draft beer. (800) 787-3982

**Range Finder Coffee** – Located inside Water Stone Outdoors, this small craft coffee bar is focused on connection and community. Their hashtag says it all: #letssteeptogether. Fair-trade certified and sustainably sourced coffee beans and loose-leaf specialty teas. (304) 574-2425

**Hawks Nest Restaurant** — Located 20 minutes from Fayetteville at Hawks Nest State Park. Features a variety of great homestyle dishes. The views from the dining room are astounding. Frequent live music and open-mic nights. 304-658-5212

**The Take-Out** — 115 E Maple Ave, near Water Stone. Serving fresh, healthy sandwiches, salads, protein and sushi bowls, powerbites, mighty muffins desserts, and daily specials like roasted-carrot "hot dogs." (304) 900-5057

## Beckley Area

Countless chain restaurants, plus some great regional and fine-dining options.

**Chilson's Grill** — Located in the historic Black Knight Country Club. Good old-fashioned home cooking: steaks, burgers, sandwiches, daily specials, desserts, and a full bar. (304) 253-7321

**Dobra Zupas** — Currently the only craft brewery in Beckley. Specialty burgers, fillet, crab risotto, plus a fresh seasonal menu. (304) 253-9872

**Fujiyama Japanese Steak House** — A casual Japanese steakhouse serving sushi, udon noodles, and hibachi-style meals. Desserts, full bar. (304) 250-0288

**Kimono Kin Japanese** — An elegant eatery offering a variety of dining experiences — a fun social hibachi, an intimate dining room, or a sushi bar. Desserts, full bar. (304) 252-2008

**King Tut Drive-In** — This family-owned business has been a locals' favorite since the 1940s. Their homemade dinner bread, bun, and pie recipes originate from Depression-era tearooms. Food is served to you by a carhop on an old-fashioned metal tray that hooks to your car window. (304) 252-6353

**Pasquale's** — Warm and relaxed atmosphere and over 50 menu items — spaghetti, lasagna, fettuccine, steaks, seafood, chicken, veal, calamari, pizza, and more. Outdoor dining available. (304) 255-5253

**Poncho & Lefty's** — Located in a converted service station. Enjoy tacos and craft beer inside or on the rooftop deck. (304) 237-1600

**Tamarack: The Best of West Virginia** — This iconic stop famous for its Appalachian crafts also features classic regional cuisine such as fried green tomatoes, pinto beans, pickled eggs, and rainbow trout. (304) 258-6843

**The Dish Café** — With themes like Pizza Wednesday, Italian Thursday, and It's Always Fresh Lunch, the menu is always interesting. The freshly made meals use natural and whole ingredients. (304) 763-2366

**The Char** — Founded in 1965, this classic steakhouse serves fine meals in an upscale setting. Escargot, shrimp cocktail, steaks, lamb chops, pastas, desserts, and a full wine list. (304) 253-1760

**Young Chow's** — The oldest continuously operating Chinese restaurant in West Virginia. Authentic favorites like egg rolls, wontons, fried rice, lo mein, egg foo young, chow mein, and more. (304) 253-5772

## Hinton Area

Hinton's small-town charm and the popularity of the nearby recreational areas supports some great restaurants — everything from diner food to classic Appalachian-inspired cuisine in a variety of casual to upscale eateries.

**Brandon's BBQ & Grill** — House-made sauces, rubs, and desserts, using fresh ingredients. Cocktails, beers, comfortable and friendly setting. (304) 466-1800

Tamarack: The Best of West Virginia.

Pop-up eats at Freefolk.

**Chessie's on the Square** — From the quilt and vintage black-and-white photo murals on the walls to the simple and tasty meals, Chessie's is all about Appalachian history. Expect a casual atmosphere with fine dining options, as well as wood-fired pizza and burgers. (304) 466-2598

**Kirk's Restaurant** — Home of the "Hungry Smile." Features an outdoor deck on the water, with diner favorites like fried fish, burgers, onion rings, turnovers, and ice cream. (304) 466-4600

**Lucky Rivers Cafe & Catering** — A casual eatery offering house-roasted coffee, soups, salads, and entrees. They have a rotating dessert menu, but staples include the Lucky Brownie and Mrs. Bengey's Lemon Ice Box Pie. (304) 445-1833

**The Market on Courthouse Square** — Soups, salads, burgers, sandwiches, pizza. (304) 466-6626

**The Oak** — Family owned and operated in a renovated rustic farmhouse that overlooks 40 acres. Fine views of the horses and farm setting. Extensive menu, with entrees from catfish to escargot. (304) 466-4800

**Tiger's Bar & Grill** — Located at Berry's Campground. Pool tables, jukebox, daily drink specials on a large covered deck on the river. Burgers, fries, salads, sandwiches, and the occasional pig roast. (304) 466-4199

## FOOD TRUCKS

### Cast Iron Smokers
Known for their out-of-this-world smoked buffalo wings, smoked mac 'n cheese, and pork nachos.
　433A Ellison Cir
　Oak Hill, WV 25901
　(304) 573-3106

### Riverchick Farm Food Truck.
Featuring vegan coconut-milk ice cream, sweet and savory crepes, and Boba teas.
　To find out where they'll be, check: www.facebook.com/Riverchick-Farm-Food-Truck-103440348054847/ (304) 877-8931

### Hot Thai Food Truck
Known for their fresh and authentic chicken panang, pad Thai, dumplings & spring rolls, noodles, and curries, you'll find this truck in Fayetteville, often by Maggie's Pub or the visitors center on Wiseman Ave.

# GYMS, YOGA, & SPAS

Sometimes, there's nothing we need more than a relaxing couple of days away from everyday life. Maybe your idea of relaxing is less about hiking or rafting and more yoga, energy work, or a spa experience. Maybe your idea of adventure is the WOD, or pumping iron in the gym. There's plenty of all of the above at the New.

## CROSSFIT, GYMS, AND INDOOR CLIMBING

When you just can't miss your WOD, stop by **BOSSMentalityCrossFit** in Oak Hill. Drop-ins are $10 for the day or buy a t-shirt for $20 and WOD for a week. bossmentalitycrossfit.com

**Active Fitness Center** features a complete workout gym, dry saunas and offers fitness classes. Drop in day passes are $10. Check out their web page for up-to-date hours and class offerings and times. activefitnessandpt.com/fitness-center/

**Outside In Climbing Gym** in Beckley features indoor bouldering and toprope climbing as well as Moonboard training. A day pass is $30 — and includes mini golf. They also have a coffee shop on-site that serves smoothies and ice cream. chocolatemoosewv.com

**CrossFit Coal** in Beckley features coached WODs and open gym times. Drop-ins are $20, or a t-shirt purchase. If you are going to drop in, email chris@crossfitcoal.com and check out WOD times at crossfitcoal.com

**Activated Body in Oak Hill** — Join a class for $15 or book a personal training/Pilates session for $60 an hour for up to three people. These sessions fill up, so book a week ahead. www.activated-body.com. They have a massage therapist on-site; reservations required.

## YOGA

Yoga is an ideal combination of physical activity and mental relaxation. The New River Gorge has several opportunities for joining in on a yoga session.

### Erin Larsen Yoga

Erin Larsen Yoga offers an in-person yoga class on Mondays from her home studio — $15 to join this 1.5-hour session. If you prefer one-on-one, that's available, and Erin also offers health coaching. www.erinlarsenyoga.com

### New River Yoga

Another great option for a relaxing yoga session: Non-members can attend classes through a donation-based system, while members can get monthly or yearly passes. Check their calendar for the most up-to-date class listings each week. www.newriveryogawv.com

## Energy Work

People carry stress in their bodies, and that stress is a form of energy. If you've never tried it, consider checking out some of the energy services offered in the New River Gorge area. Bid your anxiety farewell!

**The Reiki Training Center of West Virginia**
The Reiki Training Center of West Virginia offers multiple types of massage (including Swedish, deep tissue, neuromuscular, integrative reflexology foot, hot stone, and sports massages). You can also sign up for reiki or meditation classes. (304) 900-5066 www.thereikitrainingcenterofwv.com

**Shift Energy Work**
Want to try a non-invasive approach to healthcare? At Shift Energy Work, Kyle Rae Heeter, RN, BSN, HTP works with clients to perform gentle pain relief that complements conventional healthcare. (304) 573-4775 shiftenergywork.com

## SPAS

Treat yourself to a massage or spa session during your visit to the New River Gorge. You won't find many more tranquil activities than relaxing in a cozy spa, pampered by the professionals — ideally after a day of hiking, biking, of rafting.

### Inner Radiance Medical Spa
Inner Radiance Medical Spa on Keller Ave in Fayetteville is a medical spa that offers a variety of facials as well as massages and various aesthetic procedures like lash lifts. (681) 495-3877, innerradiancewv.com

### Canyon Massage and Bodywork
If you're in Fayetteville on a weekday, consider Canyon Massage and Bodywork for a range of therapy sessions including deep tissue, integrative, neuromuscular, and integrative reflexology for the feet. You'll need to schedule 24 hours in advance. canyonmassageandbodywork.com

### Ocean's Massage Therapy
In Oak Hill, visit Ocean's Massage Therapy at 900 Broadway. They offer a variety of therapies, including, acupressure, craniosacral therapy, moving cupping massage, massages for pregnant folks — the list goes on! www.oceansmassagetherapywv.com Email oceansmassagetherapy@gmail.com or call (304) 923-8489

### Spa Orange in Glade Springs
If you want the full spa experience, try Spa Orange for a massage, body polish, body wrap, facial, manicure, pedicure, a haircut, or all of the above. Combine it with some golf — it's at the Glade Springs Resort southeast of Beckley. (304) 763-0877, gladesprings.com/spa/

### Pipestem Spa
Near Pipestem Resort State Park south of Sandstone. With everything from a simple pedicure to the extravagant "Princess Package," you won't find yourself short on options, including body wraps, hot stone massages, distance energy healing — even bourbon tasting. (304) 466-1767

## Local Yogi

Before moving to the New River Gorge permanently, Erin Larsen was a seasonal nomad, living out of her truck. "I would make my way back to the East Coast to see family and hole up in the sleepy town of Fayetteville in the New River Gorge, and just get lost in nature, and take the time to rest and relax in this quiet place of the world."

Now a longtime Fayetteville local, Larsen offers yoga and Thai Bodywork sessions from her home studio. A yoga practitioner for 20 years and experienced bodyworker for 10 years, she says, "many people come to the New to experience all the heart-pumping adventure activities it offers, so mixing in a little restorative practice is never a bad choice." You can learn more about practicing with Larsen at **www.erinlarsenyoga.com** and check out her Airbnb yurt at **www.airbnb.com/h/nrgyurt**

# SHOPPING, ART, & EVENTS

## Mountain Momma

Candace Evans was raised in the coal fields of Logan County, WV. Her great grandmother was a pastor and her uncles were coal miners and preachers. Candace's passions are the river, the woods, yoga, photography, live music, and biking. She is married with three kids, is in love with life, and lives to laugh. She is a photographer, owner of **Thread Eclectic**, **New River Yoga**, and the event venue, **A Farm called Crowe**. "We rise by lifting others. Come visit the coolest small town." Candace masterminded our Fayetteville shopping section. You can reach her at **wvmountainmomma@hotmail.com**

Spread the love, love the spread!

## SHOPPING IN THE 'VILLE

### Thread Eclectic, Unique Boutique
New, vintage, and lightly worn clothing. Crazy stylish outfits. Games, puzzles, embroidery kits, locally made art. Find an outfit and a gift for someone without breaking the budget.

### Hobbit Hole
Retro, antique, vintage furniture. All the little knicknackpaddywhacks to make you feel nostalgic and fuzzy-like. I'll bet you can't go in there without buying something. Dare you.

### New River Bikes
Fayetteville's full-service bike shop. No matter what kind of riding you're into, be it riding around town or riding wheelies they have you covered. Whether you need a tube, service, rentals, or a guided tour, they'll keep you rolling.

### Twisted Gypsy's
Located at 102 Wiseman Ave, this hip shop is filled with fun boho apparel and gifts. www.facebook/twistedgypsys.com

### Wild Art, Wonderful Things
Over 15 local artisans represented. Always something new and fresh. Find a gift for your momma or buy a pair of earrings for yourself.

### Great Googly Moogly
For rock and gem hounds — everything from beautifully wrapped stones to prayer flags. Their rock collection is to die for.

### Very Rare Vintage
Eclectic and cool vintage shop, with an incredible selection of classic t-shirts.

### Ben Franklin
Rocking Fayetteville's needs for 60 years! Anything from fresh-ground peanuts to fabric.

## Water Stone Outdoors
A cornerstone of downtown Fayetteville. Climbing store with a plethora of climbing and paddling gear and name-brand outdoor clothing. Excellent selection and extremely knowledgeable staff. Also home to Range Finder Coffee and New River Mountain Guides.

## Wisteria's Gifts
Featuring unique jewelry, beads, Vera Bradley, WV gourmet foods and wines, candles, home décor, and more.

## New River Antique Mall
A block off Court St, south of Water Stone. Different vendors featuring a wide variety of wares. You can always find something fun to add to your collectibles.

## Out of the Ashes
Near the courthouse. New women's clothing and Fayetteville pillows and gifts.

## Studio B.
North end of Keller Ave. Local t-shirts and stickers. Top-notch booze, cheese, mustards, jewelry, and smiles.

## ACE Gear Shop
You can buy anything from socks to boats.

## Dove's Village
Off US 19 south of Fayetteville. Featuring carefully curated rustic, vintage, and farmhouse decor for over 45 years, Dove's has a unique selection of gifts, craft and wares.
www.dovesvillage.com

## Love Hope Center for the Arts
Far south end of Court St. Dedicated to enhancing the arts in central Appalachia and provides an educational art space for the New River Gorge area. They have an exhibition space, retail, and education center.
www.lovehopearts.org

## Canyon Rim Gifts
Located just east of the Canyon Rim Visitor Center parking. From hand-dipped ice cream to melt-in-your-mouth fudge, rocks, fossils, and NRG souvenirs, gifts, and t-shirts, plan to spend time at this fun shop.

## Tamarack Marketplace
Located right off I-64/77 at exit 45 just north of Beckley. Features West Virginia's best Appalachian artistry, in an iconic peak-roofed building. You can shop the arts and crafts of over 2800 artists and artisans from all 55 WV counties at this regional showcase. Shopping, plus a summer concert series and Appalachian cuisine restaurants, and artist demonstrations.

## Mountain Home Metalworks
Fine craft metalware for kitchen and home, forged in the hill of West Virginia. Featuring beautiful designs and skilled craftsmanship, Mountain Home Metal Works has a full line of hand-crafted metalware.
www.mountainhomemetalworks.com

# EVENTS

One thing they really know how to do in the New is throw an event, from **Harry Potter-themed Wizard Weekend** in January to the weekly **Pun n Play** at the Gaines Estate, **Very Rare Vintage's Vintage Clothing and Arts Festival** in June, to Drag Shows and Comedy Nights at the Southside Junction Tap House. You will find endless options for festive visits in Fayetteville. Visit visitfayettevillewv.com for up-to-date listings of events in Fayetteville.

In Beckley you can attend the annual **Appalachian Arts and Crafts fair** in August or The **Annual Chili Night** in downtown Beckley in October. For more events and up-to-date info visit www.raleighcountyevents.com.

In Hinton you can enjoy **Pipestem's Summer Amphitheater Series**, the **Fear Fest** in July, and guided hikes and flea markets. Visit www.exploresummerscounty.com/events for more listings.

## Gauley Season

Each year, water lovers across the nation look forward to Gauley Season, a controlled release of the Summersville Lake waters that turns the Gauley River into one of the best whitewater rivers in the world. Beginning the second week of September, visitors can expect a flow of approximately 2800 cubic feet per second on certain Fridays, Saturdays, Sundays, and Mondays during the two-month release. That means big water and lots of fun and antics on the river. Around 44,000 people from all corners of the world raft the river during Gauley Season. Think you're ready to experience the "Beast of the East" yourself? Do it!

Bridge Day BASE jumping. 📷 Jay Young

## Bridge Day

Held annually since 1980, this event has been a go-to destination for extreme-sports enthusiasts from all over the planet. It's the largest event of its type in the country. Every third Saturday in October, US 19 across the New River Gorge Bridge is closed to traffic and the bridge becomes a pedestrian mall and event venue. The main event is BASE jumping — watch skilled skydivers leap off the bridge, pop their chutes, and glide smoothly down to the beach (or sometimes into the water, to be retrieved by waiting rescue teams).

Athletes from dozens of states and multiple countries take part in the event to show off their skills and have fun performing flips and other athletic feats. Around 80,000 people come to the event each year, so you'll likely make even more friends than you bring. In 2019, the event saw:

- 303 BASE jumpers
- 910 rappelers
- 790 jumps

officialbridgeday.com

## New and Scary

A unique website for NRG/monster-themed stuff, from the imagination of local wizard Jay Young. Featuring fun monsters created by West Virginia artists, gracing t-shirts, coffee mugs, and other assorted merch. Men's, women's, kid's, and baby sizes — unique souvenirs all, and you don't even have to be in the New to get them.
MonstersWV.com

### Homoclimbtastic

The world's largest gathering of LGBTQ rock climbers (and friends!), the HomoClimbtastic Climbing Convention was founded in 2007, and is held annually in late July in Fayetteville. The town really throws down for this flamboyant, rainbow event.

📷 Karen Lane

## MUSIC FESTIVALS

Music brings people together to generally have a good old time. Festivalnet.com/West-Virginia-music-festivals has tickets and up-to-date listings.

### New River Gorge Festival

This three-day festival is held annually in May at ACE Adventure Resort. A full lineup of outdoor adventures, camping, and live music.

### Mountain Music Festival

Held annually in early June at ACE, this festival features live performances by well-known favorites and up-and-coming artists.

### Appalachian String Band Music Festival

Held in August at Camp Washington Carver near Babcock State Park southeast of Fayetteville (on-site camping available). Get ready to be a part of the music, with square dances, workshops, hymn-sings, and contests.

### Live Music Wednesdays at the Gaines Estate

Wednesday from 4 to 10PM you can experience a family friendly mini-fest at the Gaines Estate in Fayetteville. Food, yard games, and live music make for laughter and dancing. www.gainesestate.com (304) 382-7509

## Hank Williams' Last Stop

Hank Williams was one of the most significant and influential American singers and songwriters of the 20th century. He recorded 55 singles that reached the top 10 of the Billboard Country & Western chart, with 12 of his songs reaching number 1. Early on New Years day, 1953, Hank Williams died from a heart attack in the back of Cadillac, while on his way to a gig. The driver had stopped at the Skyline Drive-In in Hilltop to use the restroom, then he discovered that Hank had died. Known today as "Hank's Last Stop," the Skyline Drive-in is still a popular stop.

# Mountain Sounds

## BY LEWIS RHINEHART

**The West Virginia music scene** is incredibly vibrant and is a direct reflection of the talented people who comprise its rich history and its current far-reaching sounds. Musicians from around the globe have contributed to what has become a music of many names: Mountain Music, Bluegrass, Folk. The vocals of church and gospel music, the high-lonesome sound of the mandolin, influenced by Italian and Celtic stringed instruments and harmonica and banjo sounds bringing the lament of African slaves from the southern US all add up to a distinctly "West Virginia" sound. Each of these bands and places are unique in their own way while still remaining true to themes that run deep in the culture, people, and music of West Virginia music. A fierce do-it-yourself attitude, a reverence for our history and hope for the future.

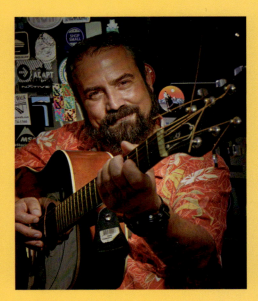

Top local bands include:

- **The Kind Thieves** — Appalachian Jamgrass? Mountain Rock? Psychedelic JamFunk? YOU try to classify them after seeing one of their incendiary live shows. **@thekindthieves**

- **Matt Mullins and the Bringdowns** — Intermittently raw, rocking, funny, poignant, clever, and always in homage to West Virginia history. **www.bringdowns.com**

- **Andrew Adkins & Friends** — Foot-stomping musical love letters to the hollers of WV. Gospel rave-ups, country-tinged observations of our current Appalachian landscape (the good and the bad), and tips of the hat to the musical traditions that make up today's Appalachian sound. **www.andrewadkinswv.com**

Jay Young

Take some time, dig into West Virginia music, and catch these artists around the New at The Burrito Bar at Breeze Hill, Our House at Cantrell's, Freefolk Brewery, Rendezvous River Lodge, South Side Junction and Tap House, Arrowhead Bike Farm, and the Gaines Estate.